CGP
– books
like no others!

CGP

It's another Quality Book from CGP

This book is for 7-11 year olds.

Whatever subject you're doing it's the same
old story — there are lots of facts and you've just got
to learn them. KS2 English is no different.

Happily this CGP book gives you all that important
information as clearly and concisely as possible.

It's also got some daft bits in to try and make the whole
experience at least vaguely entertaining for you.

What CGP is all about

Our sole aim here at CGP is to produce the highest quality books
— carefully written, immaculately presented and dangerously
close to being funny.

Then we work our socks off to get them out to you
— at the cheapest possible prices.

Contents

Published by CGP

From original material by Richard Parsons.

Contributors:
Simon Cook
Chris Dennett
Gemma Hallam
Simon Little
Glenn Rogers
Camilla Simson
Kate Stevens
Claire Thompson
Tim Wakeling
James Paul Wallis
Ruth Wilbourne

ISBN: 978 1 84146 150 2

Story on p52: all-new original adaptation of a medieval folk legend.
Poem on p58: *Windy Nights* by Robert Louis Stevenson.

Groovy website: www.cgpbooks.co.uk
Jolly bits of clipart from CorelDRAW®
Printed by Elanders Ltd, Newcastle upon Tyne.

Nouns

Any word that means a <u>thing</u> (like a person, an animal, a place, or even a turnip) is called a <u>noun</u>.

Nouns are words for Things

In other words, <u>nouns</u> are just the <u>names</u> of things.
Here are a few everyday ones:

> ### man, tree, hedgehog, balloon

It could also be the name of something like a <u>person</u>, a <u>place</u>, a <u>day</u> or a <u>month</u>. Watch out though — these always have a <u>capital letter</u>...

> ### Steve, France, Monday, September

Those are names of types of things or a single thing, but words for <u>groups</u> of things are also nouns:

> ### herd, flock, team, bundle

You need to put '<u>the</u>', '<u>a</u>', or '<u>an</u>' in front of some nouns — these words are called <u>articles</u>. They show if you're talking about something <u>generally</u>, e.g. '<u>a</u> tree', or if you are talking about a <u>particular</u> thing, e.g. '<u>the</u> tree'.

Not All Nouns are things you can Touch

Be careful though — some nouns are names of those weird things that you <u>can't see</u>, <u>touch</u> or <u>hear</u>:

Grrr!

> Just <u>remember</u> that these things are still <u>nouns</u>. It's so easy to forget.

> ### love, freedom, sleep, life, truth, anger

Noun — not the middle of the day...

It'll be much easier later on if you know what a noun is. So learn the four kinds now: 1) a type of <u>thing</u>, 2) a single <u>thing</u>, 3) a <u>group</u> of things, 4) a <u>thing</u> even if you can't touch it (an idea).

Pronouns

Look at this — <u>Fred</u> said that <u>Fred</u> was going to <u>Fred's</u> house. That sounds <u>rubbish</u>.
It'd be stacks <u>better</u> to use words like '<u>he</u>' and '<u>his</u>' because it would be much less <u>boring</u>.

Don't keep Repeating the same long Words

Take a look at these sentences, and I'll show you what I mean:

① *Rachel took an apple. <u>Rachel</u> ate the <u>apple</u> on the way to school.*

Instead of saying '<u>Rachel</u>' again, I've written '<u>she</u>'.

Instead of saying '<u>apple</u>' again, I've written '<u>it</u>'.

② *Rachel took an apple. <u>She</u> ate <u>it</u> on the way to school.*

It <u>sounds much better</u> with the '<u>she</u>' and '<u>it</u>' in this sentence.

Which Pronoun Depends on Who's Doing the Action

I bet you already <u>knew</u> all the pronouns, even if you didn't know they were <u>called</u> pronouns.
The trouble is though, <u>which</u> one you use depends <u>what they're doing</u> in the sentence:

Only use these for something that is <u>doing</u> the action in a sentence.

Only use these for something that is having the action <u>done to it</u>.

These ones <u>don't change</u>, so they're dead easy.

<u>you</u> ➡ <u>you</u>
<u>it</u> ➡ <u>it</u>

<u>I</u> ➡ <u>me</u>
<u>he</u> ➡ <u>him</u>
<u>she</u> ➡ <u>her</u>
<u>we</u> ➡ <u>us</u>
<u>they</u> ➡ <u>them</u>

I was <u>doing</u> the action in the sentence. You can't say 'Me was'.

<u>I</u> was chasing the giant pineapple.
The giant pineapple was chasing <u>me</u>.

I was having the action <u>done to me</u> in this sentence. You can't say 'chasing I'.

Pronouns

Don't go crashing straight in, you've got to use the <u>right</u> word in the <u>right</u> place. Here's what to do.

Getting Them and They the Right Way Round

It's so easy to get words like '<u>them</u>' and '<u>they</u>' the <u>wrong</u> way round. Most of the time though you should be able to tell by how it <u>sounds</u>.

This is <u>doing</u> the action in the sentence, so we must use 'they'. You can't say 'Them ate'.

They ate the killer cheesecake.
The killer cheesecake ate <u>them</u>.

This is having the action <u>done to it</u>, so we must use 'them'. You can't say 'ate they'.

I, He, She, We and They

Arthur had a seriously cool yo-yo.

'<u>Arthur</u>' is replaced by '<u>he</u>'. You can't write 'Him had'.

He had a seriously cool yo-yo.

<u>The lifeguards</u> are practising their dance.

There's <u>more than one</u> lifeguard, so we must use 'them' or 'they'. They're <u>doing</u> the action (dancing), so we use '<u>they</u>'.

<u>They</u> are practising their dance.

That noun's great — he's a real pro...

<u>Not</u> the hardest thing in the world, this. You probably already know <u>most</u> of what's on these two pages. Make <u>doubly sure</u> that you know it <u>all</u> — a few measly <u>mistakes</u> and you'll lose <u>marks</u>.

Adjectives

Adjectives <u>describe things</u> and tell you more about them. They make your writing more <u>interesting</u>.

Adjectives Describe Nouns

Some sentences are really <u>dull</u> like this one:

The caterpillar wore socks.   Really dull.

<u>Adjectives</u> help you <u>jazz up</u> your sentences — they're <u>describing words</u> that give you a <u>better picture</u> of the things they describe. Here's the same sentence with some <u>adjectives</u> thrown in:

The <u>hairy green</u> caterpillar wore <u>baggy pink</u> socks.

Hairy and green are <u>adjectives</u>.
They <u>describe</u> the caterpillar.

Baggy and pink are <u>adjectives</u>.
They <u>describe</u> the socks.

Not just any old socks, but baggy pink ones...

An Adjective can go Before or After a Noun

Adjectives can go <u>before</u> a noun like this:

The fish band played <u>beautiful</u> music.

They can also go <u>after</u> a noun like this...

The wizard's lunch smells <u>disgusting</u>.

...and this.

The present was <u>huge</u> and <u>blue</u>.

Season with plenty of adjectives before serving...

No-one wants to read <u>boring</u> sentences, so make sure you liven things up with some well-chosen <u>adjectives</u>. It'll make your writing loads more <u>exciting</u>, and help you pick up those juicy marks...

Verbs

As you're <u>reading</u> this book, I bet you <u>wish</u> you were out <u>playing</u> football or <u>riding</u> your bike, or <u>eating</u> your dinner, or <u>watching</u> the TV. If you hadn't guessed it yet, <u>verbs</u> are '<u>action</u>' words.

Most Verbs are 'Doing' Words

Here's a nice, easy rule to learn. It's very simple — whenever you write a sentence it must have at least one <u>action word</u> in it. This action word is called a <u>verb</u>.

Henry <u>surfed</u> into a giant cucumber.

These are the <u>verbs</u>. Some verbs are made of <u>two separate words</u>.

Emily <u>is eating</u> a turnip.

Some Verbs are 'Being' words

This can be a bit confusing. Nearly all verbs are <u>action</u> words like the ones above, but there are a few that are '<u>being</u>' words. They tell you <u>about</u> something, instead of what it is <u>doing</u>.

The surgeon <u>is</u> ready for the operation.

The men <u>were</u> very old.

The main thing to remember is that these are still <u>verbs</u>, even though they are <u>not</u> really '<u>action</u>' words.

I <u>am</u> cold.

Come on — I want to see some action...

There it is then — a <u>verb</u> is just an <u>action</u> word or a <u>being</u> word. Without a verb, it's not a proper sentence. It's as simple as that. And whatever you do, don't forget the <u>capital letter</u> and <u>full stop</u>.

Adverbs

Think you've got adjectives and verbs sorted? Goodo, then it's time for <u>adverbs</u>.
These are words that are used to <u>describe verbs</u>. They say <u>how</u> something was <u>done</u>.

Adverbs Describe Verbs

Adverbs tell you <u>how</u> a verb was <u>done</u>. Most of them end in '<u>-ly</u>'.

The zoo keeper <u>quickly</u> <u>ran</u> away from the lion.

This is the <u>adverb</u>.
It describes the verb 'ran' — it
says <u>how</u> the zoo keeper ran away.

This is the <u>verb</u>.

Some <u>adjectives</u>, like 'lovely'
and 'friendly' end in '-ly' as
well. Watch out for them
— they <u>aren't adverbs</u>.

The dragon <u>played</u> his guitar <u>loudly</u>.

This is the <u>verb</u>.

This is the <u>adverb</u>.
It describes <u>how</u> the
dragon played the guitar.

Adverbs Make Your Writing Better

Adverbs make your sentences more <u>interesting</u> and <u>descriptive</u>.

The striker headed the ball.

The striker <u>fearlessly</u> headed the ball.

This sentence sounds
loads better now — it's
more <u>exciting</u> to read.

The gardener approached the carrot.

The gardener approached the carrot <u>nervously</u>.

We've 'ad verbs, now we're onto adverbs...

Adverbs are a way to <u>spice things up</u> and make what's happening in your writing really <u>clear</u>.
Pick them carefully and you'll paint your reader a lovely detailed picture of what's going on.

Prepositions

Prepositions show what's <u>under</u> what, who's <u>next to</u> who, what's <u>where</u> and what's <u>when</u>. My, that didn't sound in the <u>least</u> bit confusing... Read on, and all will be made crystal clear.

Prepositions Can Tell You Where Things Are

<u>Prepositions</u> are words and phrases like '<u>under</u>', '<u>in front of</u>', '<u>between</u>' and '<u>with</u>'. They tell you how <u>nouns</u> (or pronouns) are <u>related</u> to each other.

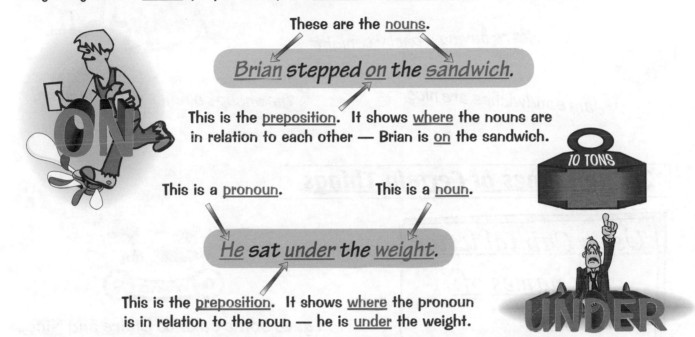

These are the <u>nouns</u>.

<u>Brian</u> stepped <u>on</u> the <u>sandwich</u>.

This is the <u>preposition</u>. It shows <u>where</u> the nouns are in relation to each other — Brian is <u>on</u> the sandwich.

This is a <u>pronoun</u>.   This is a <u>noun</u>.

<u>He</u> sat <u>under</u> the <u>weight</u>.

This is the <u>preposition</u>. It shows <u>where</u> the pronoun is in relation to the noun — he is <u>under</u> the weight.

There are plenty <u>more</u> prepositions out there. The <u>best</u> way to spot one is to ask yourself if it tells you about the <u>relation</u> between two things. If it <u>does</u>, then it's a <u>preposition</u>.

Prepositions are about Time as well as Place

Prepositions can tell you about <u>when</u> things are as well as <u>where</u> they are.

Let's go for a coffee <u>after</u> work.

Carrie got to the dinosaurs <u>before</u> Paul.

Hassan span round and round <u>until</u> midnight.

Uncomfortable? Get into a better preposition...

<u>Preposition</u>, eh? It's another of those <u>stonking</u> great long names for measly little words. There's no point in <u>complaining</u>, you know. They're called prepositions, and that's that. Isn't this <u>fun</u>?

| CAPITAL LETTERS & FULL STOPS | **Stopping and Starting a Sentence** |

These pages tell you <u>how to start and end a sentence</u> and when to use <u>CAPITAL LETTERS</u>...

Capital Letters are used for...

1) The Start of a Sentence

All sentences <u>start</u> with a <u>capital letter</u>.

Examples

<u>W</u>e're having a party tonight.

<u>J</u>am sandwiches are nice.

<u>T</u>he sheep couldn't stop laughing.

2) The Names of Certain Things

Use a Capital letter for names of:

1) <u>People</u>
2) <u>People's titles</u>
3) <u>Places</u>
4) <u>Days of the week</u>
5) <u>Months of the year</u>
6) <u>Organisations</u>

EXAMPLES

I gave some cake to <u>Claire</u> and <u>Nicola</u>.

I have an appointment with <u>Dr Jekyll</u>.

I went to <u>York</u> last week.

My sister is coming to dinner on <u>Thursday</u>.

<u>Lauren</u> is going to <u>Spain</u> in <u>July</u>.

I support <u>Leicester City</u>.

Most Sentences End with a Full Stop

You need a <u>full stop</u> to show that your <u>sentence is finished</u>. Most sentences that end in a <u>full stop</u> are <u>statements</u> — they tell you <u>facts</u>.

EXAMPLE

A full stop goes here.

<u>P</u>aula caught an electric eel in her eel trap. <u>S</u>he cut it into bits and fed it to the cat.

Begin with a capital letter.

A capital letter begins the next sentence.

Another full stop goes here.

Special Sentences — ? and !

Question marks and exclamation marks are the handsome wee devils that can go at the end of a sentence instead of a full stop.

Question Marks are used for Questions

You have to use these for question sentences.

Any sentence asking a question must end with a question mark instead of a full stop.

Where do you keep the seagulls?
What are you doing to my neck?

Put a question mark instead of a full stop.

Exclamation Marks are used for...

1) Exclamations

This groovy symbol is an exclamation mark.

Exclamation marks replace the full stop in sentences which show really strong feelings.

English is brilliant!

It's awful!   *What a great day!*   *Oh no!*
Mayonnaise is the worst!   *I can't believe it!*

2) Commands

A command is a sentence that tells someone to do something.

You can tell if a sentence is a command because it always has an imperative in it. An imperative is a verb used to give an order.

Go away!
Be quiet!
Get out!

These are imperatives.
Stop it!
Stand still!
Close the door!

Commands often have exclamation marks, but sometimes they just have full stops.

Tests — they're a question of marks...

This stuff isn't easy, but with a smidgen of effort you can make your writing loads better. Use a '?' every time the sentence asks a question, and only use one '!' for exclamations and commands.

APOSTROPHES

Showing Who Owns What

Apostrophes are the little comma-shaped squiggles used to show when something belongs to somebody. Learn all about them or you'll make dead nasty mistakes.

Adding 's to show Who Owns What

> To show that something belongs to a person, you take their name and add an apostrophe and an 's'.

Kylie's hair is bright green.

Sophie's mice have grown very fat.

If the name already ends with an 's', you can either add an apostrophe and another 's', or just add an apostrophe:

> *James's bike has been flattened.*
>
> *Magnus' dog has got fleas.*

Watch out, though. Some names are only written one way. All you can do is learn them, I'm afraid.

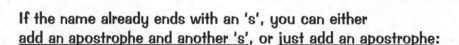

Jesus' disciples   St James's Park

For Groups of People...

If it's a word for a group of people or a group of things which ends in 's', all you do is stick an apostrophe on the end.

I guess they needed a wash...

> *I washed the neighbours' windows with orangeade.*

Words like men, women and children are easy because they don't end in 's'. Just add an apostrophe and an 's'.

> *I put the men's shoes in the toilet and the women's shoes in the pond.*

You can have the cat, but the apostrophe's mine...

It doesn't get much simpler than this. You use apostrophe "s" unless it's a plural that ends in "s". Life couldn't be quite that simple of course, there are those pesky exceptions that need learning.

Show Missing Letters with an '

When you shove two words <u>together</u>, you stick in an <u>apostrophe</u> to show where you've <u>missed out</u> letters. <u>Easy-peasy</u> I'd say — just ready for seizing juicy <u>marks</u>. Learn <u>how</u> to do it <u>now</u>.

Making Two words into One

The <u>apostrophe</u> goes <u>in place</u> of the letters that have been <u>missed out</u>. You use this to write the short, <u>casual</u> forms of words that people use when they <u>talk</u>. Learn the ones in the table.

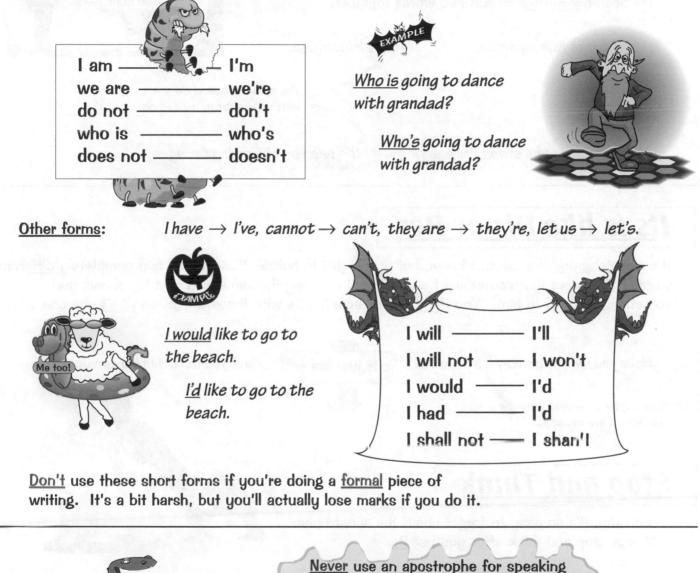

I am —— I'm
we are —— we're
do not —— don't
who is —— who's
does not —— doesn't

EXAMPLE

<u>Who is</u> going to dance with grandad?

<u>Who's</u> going to dance with grandad?

<u>Other forms:</u> I have → I've, cannot → can't, they are → they're, let us → let's.

Me too!

<u>I would</u> like to go to the beach.

<u>I'd</u> like to go to the beach.

I will —— I'll
I will not —— I won't
I would —— I'd
I had —— I'd
I shall not —— I shan'l

<u>Don't</u> use these short forms if you're doing a <u>formal</u> piece of writing. It's a bit harsh, but you'll actually lose marks if you do it.

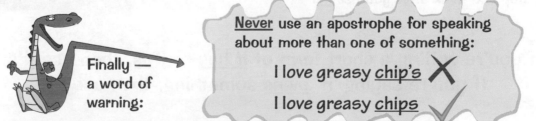

Finally — a word of warning:

<u>Never</u> use an apostrophe for speaking about more than one of something:

I love greasy <u>chip's</u> ✗

I love greasy <u>chips</u> ✓

Missing letters? — see your postman...

Don't forget to leave a wee <u>gap</u> and bung in your <u>apostrophe</u> when there are letters <u>missing</u>. You'll lose <u>marks</u> if you <u>don't</u> and your writing won't be <u>clear</u> — for example <u>he'll</u> = he will, <u>hell</u> = fire and brimstone. ...And get this between your ears: never <u>EVER</u> use <u>'s</u> for a bog standard <u>plural</u>.

IT'S AND ITS

Don't Confuse It's and Its

You wouldn't think that two <u>spiddly little words</u> could cause so much <u>hassle</u>. Avoid <u>mistakes</u> and pick up more glorious <u>marks</u> — by <u>learning</u> the difference between <u>it's</u> and <u>its</u>. What fun.

It's means 'it is' Or 'it has'

<u>It's</u> means <u>it is</u> or <u>it has</u>, and <u>nothing else</u>. The <u>apostrophe</u> is there to show that a letter has been <u>missed out</u> to run two words together.

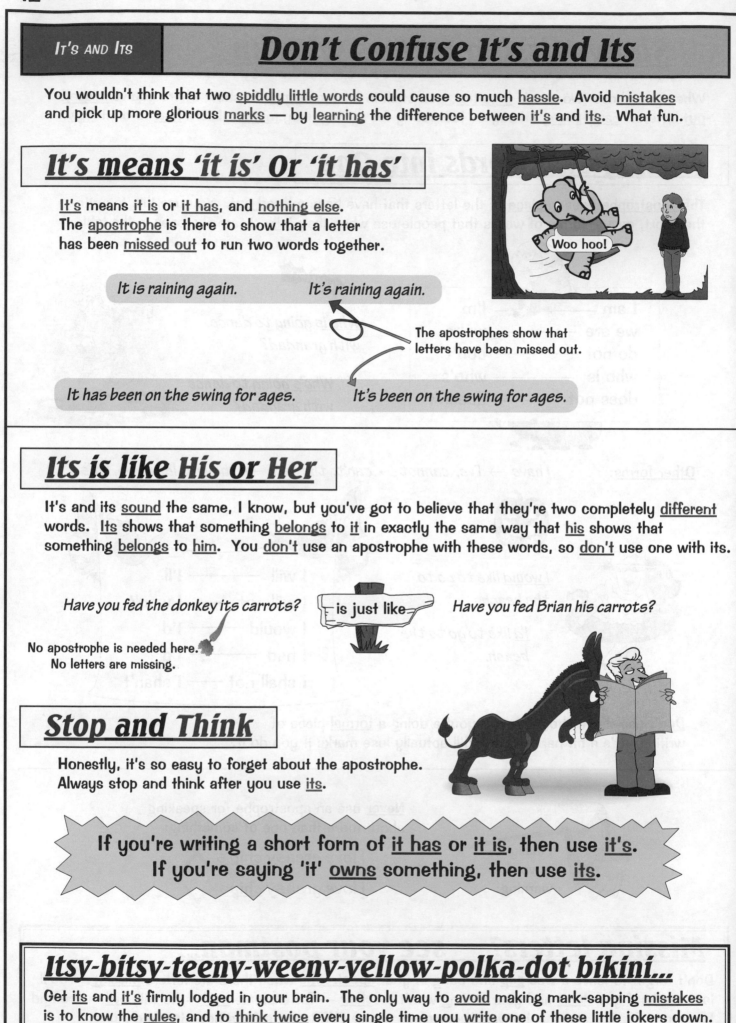

Woo hoo!

It is raining again.   It's raining again.

The apostrophes show that letters have been missed out.

It has been on the swing for ages.   It's been on the swing for ages.

Its is like His or Her

<u>It's</u> and its <u>sound</u> the same, I know, but you've got to believe that they're two completely <u>different</u> words. <u>Its</u> shows that something <u>belongs</u> to <u>it</u> in exactly the same way that <u>his</u> shows that something <u>belongs</u> to <u>him</u>. You <u>don't</u> use an apostrophe with these words, so <u>don't</u> use one with its.

Have you fed the donkey its carrots?   is just like   Have you fed Brian his carrots?

No apostrophe is needed here. No letters are missing.

Stop and Think

Honestly, it's so easy to forget about the apostrophe. Always stop and think after you use <u>its</u>.

If you're writing a short form of <u>it has</u> or <u>it is</u>, then use <u>it's</u>. If you're saying 'it' <u>owns</u> something, then use <u>its</u>.

Itsy-bitsy-teeny-weeny-yellow-polka-dot bikini...

Get <u>its</u> and <u>it's</u> firmly lodged in your brain. The only way to <u>avoid</u> making mark-sapping <u>mistakes</u> is to know the <u>rules</u>, and to <u>think twice</u> every single time you <u>write</u> one of these little jokers down.

Commas — Lists & Long Sentences

Commas are dead <u>important</u>. If you use them in <u>lists</u>, and to break up <u>long</u> sentences, you'll make your writing <u>clearer</u> and easier to read — and that means bags more <u>marks</u>. Learn all about it.

Commas are used Between items in a List

When you have a list, you <u>must</u> use commas. Don't worry, it's a breeze if you <u>learn the rules</u>:

Using Commas in Lists

1) Put a <u>comma</u> after every word in the list <u>except the last one</u>.

2) Put an '<u>and</u>' or an '<u>or</u>' between the last two words.

I didn't know whether to laugh, cry or scream.

The monster was huge, ugly, smelly and angry.

Now this bit's a tad tricky, so get it firmly lodged in your brain:

If the <u>last two items</u> in the list <u>already</u> have 'and' between them, you need to stick a <u>comma</u> and an '<u>and</u>' before them.

We had pizza, sausages, and steak and chips.

It needs this comma to separate the 'sausages' from the 'steak and chips'.

Commas can make the Meaning more Clear

And there's more, hurrah! We also need commas in long sentences to break them up.

Commas break up long sentences to make them <u>easier to understand</u>.

① Commas break up sentences where <u>more than one thing happens</u>.

Andy knocked on the door several times, but nobody answered.

I'm in the toilet, you'll have to wait.

WHY WILL NOBODY ANSWER THE DOOR?

② Commas break up sentences when <u>extra information is given</u> about something.

With a squeak, the squirrel pounced on the giraffe.

Commas — not full stops with beards...

Commas in <u>lists</u> are pretty <u>easy</u>, but the <u>last two</u> items need thinking about.
Commas in <u>long sentences</u> are a bit more grisly, but they're definitely worth <u>learning</u>.

| SPEECH MARKS | # Show When People Speak With "" |

Don't be scared of speech marks. They're not exactly easy, but if you learn <u>all</u> the <u>rules</u> and use them properly in your <u>writing</u>, you'll open the door to a great dollop of <u>marks</u>. Learn and <u>practise</u> pal.

Speech Marks show when Someone is Speaking

This stuff's very easy to get wrong. The secret to success is learning all the rules:

RULE 1 Put speech marks around the <u>actual words</u> that are spoken.

Use a capital letter when someone starts to speak. **RULE 2**

Put a comma <u>before</u> the speech starts.

A capital letter goes here.

FOR EXAMPLE

Kelly said, "Strawberry milkshakes are really lush."

Speech marks open the actual speech...   ...and speech marks close it again.

Use a Comma if...

RULE 3 If the whole sentence ends when the speech ends, put a <u>full stop</u> before the closing speech mark.

Bob said, "We're going on a treasure hunt."

RULE 4 If the sentence continues after the speech, put a <u>comma</u> before the closing speech mark.

"I think that we should take some cake with us," he said.

A New Speaker needs a New Line...

RULE 5 When a new person speaks, start on a new line.

Jenny's speech starts on a new line.

"Do you like football?" asked Chris.
"No, I only like worms," Jenny replied.

Speech marks — six out of ten?...

Remember to use speech marks when someone <u>starts</u> to <u>speak</u>, and again when they <u>stop</u> talking. Stick a <u>new speaker</u> on a <u>new line</u> and don't forget those <u>tricky</u> bits about <u>commas</u> and <u>capitals</u>.

When to Use Speech Marks

It's not enough to know <u>how</u> speech marks work. You can't just <u>bung</u> them anywhere. You've got to use them in the <u>right place</u>.

When to use Speech Marks...

This is the most important bit about writing speech. Get this sorted and you're away.

Use speech marks when you write the <u>exact words</u> spoken.

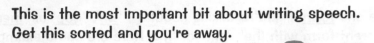

These are the exact words Ali said, so we must use speech marks.

"Where have my rabbits gone?" asked Ali.

The sentence could have said this instead:

Ali asked where his rabbits had gone.

We call this <u>reported speech</u> — it's when the writer tells you in his own words what was said.

Speech marks aren't used here because the <u>SENTENCE DOESN'T USE THE ACTUAL WORDS</u> that Ali said.

Only when the Exact Words are used...

<u>Never ever</u> use speech marks for reported speech (when you're not using the exact words of the person speaking). It's wrong, and you'll lose precious marks if you do this.

Jess' exact words aren't used here, so we don't want speech marks.

Jess said that she wanted to go on the roller coaster again.

Jess said <u>I want to go on the roller coaster again.</u>

These are her exact words, so they need speech marks around them.

Jess said, "I want to go on the roller coaster again."

Speech marks mark speech in Mark's speech...

This whole page is about using speech marks <u>if</u> and <u>only if</u> you're writing out the <u>exact words</u> spoken. Get <u>that</u> into your head. If it's <u>reported speech</u>, you <u>don't</u> need speech marks.

| VERBS | ## Using Verbs in Sentences |

Verbs are 'doing' or 'being' words, and every sentence has one. But it's not just choosing which verb goes in a sentence that matters — you've got to get the verbs in the right form too.

The Form of a Verb Shows Who's Doing the Action

Most verbs have one form if you're talking about 'I', 'we', 'you' or 'they', but they have a different form with 'he', 'she' or 'it'. Here are some examples...

> To remind yourself about verbs, see p.5.

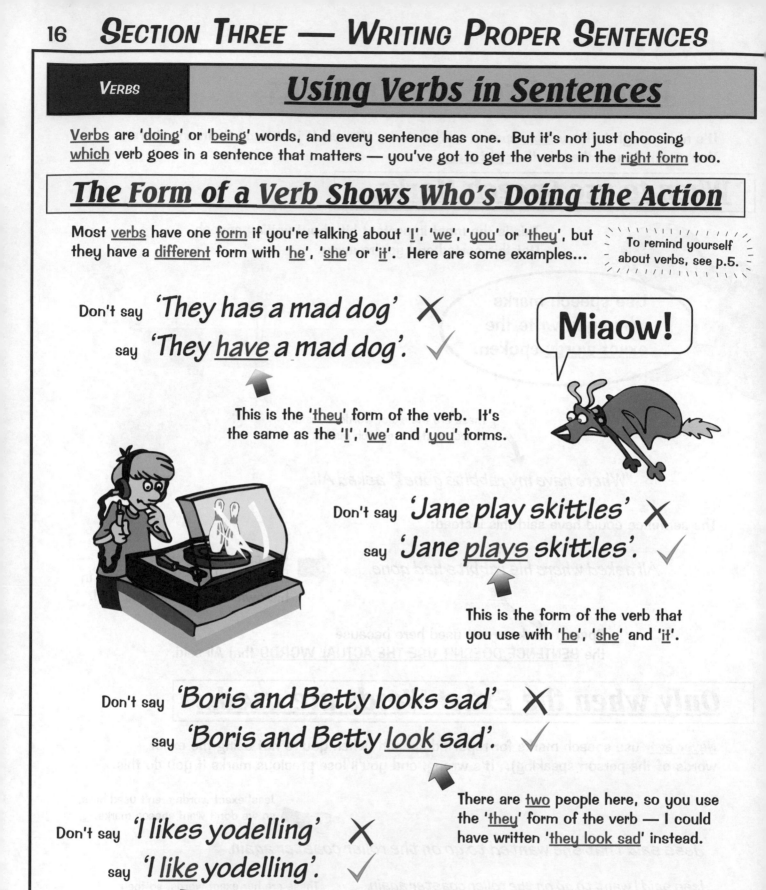

Don't say *'They has a mad dog'* ✗
say *'They have a mad dog'.* ✓

This is the 'they' form of the verb. It's the same as the 'I', 'we' and 'you' forms.

Miaow!

Don't say *'Jane play skittles'* ✗
say *'Jane plays skittles'.* ✓

This is the form of the verb that you use with 'he', 'she' and 'it'.

Don't say *'Boris and Betty looks sad'* ✗
'Boris and Betty look sad'. ✓

There are two people here, so you use the 'they' form of the verb — I could have written 'they look sad' instead.

Don't say *'I likes yodelling'* ✗
say *'I like yodelling'.* ✓

The 'I' form of the verb — the same as the 'we', 'you' and 'they' forms.

Changing forms — I used to be in class 3B...

Don't stuff the action word in any old how — you've got to make it work with the thing that's doing it... in other words, don't write "you is" or "they wants" or anything daft like that.

Verb Tenses

Verbs have a tense. This tells you about when the action happens. Or when it happened. Or when it will happen. It sounds kind of tricky, but you do it every day when you talk to people.

The Tense of a Verb Tells You When it Happens

Verbs describe the action in the sentence. Of course, the action can happen at different times — in the past, the present or the future. This changes the tense of the verb.

Bruce <u>played</u> basketball for Astro United.

Bruce used to play in the <u>PAST</u>.

Bruce <u>plays</u> basketball for Astro United.

Bruce is playing now, in the <u>PRESENT</u>.

Bruce <u>will play</u> basketball for Astro United.

Bruce is going to play in the <u>FUTURE</u>.

Watch Out for Tenses that Don't Make Sense

Using the wrong tense can make you lose marks. Fast. Look out for sentences like these, where the verbs are in the wrong tense...

Richard will cleaned his desk tomorrow. ✗

Richard will <u>clean</u> his desk tomorrow. ✓

The sausage is winning the chess match yesterday. ✗

The sausage <u>won</u> the chess match yesterday. ✓

The doctor wants to ate all of my grapes. ✗

The doctor wants to <u>eat</u> all of my grapes. ✓

If you want your sentence to make sense...

... make sure your verb is in the right tense. Now that's a handy little rhyme to remember...

Comparing Things Properly

<u>Comparisons</u> are a brilliant way of grabbing people's <u>attention</u>. Don't say you're <u>funny</u> — say you're <u>funnier</u> than a clown convention. Read this page and you'll be <u>cleverer</u> than... well, before you read it.

Two Smashing Ways to Compare things

① For short words like '<u>tall</u>', '<u>short</u>', '<u>high</u>' and '<u>low</u>' — you add '<u>-er than</u>'.

Sam is tall<u>er than</u> Ellie.

② For all other comparisons, use '<u>more</u>', '<u>less</u>' or '<u>as</u>', like these:

Betty is <u>more</u> beautiful <u>than</u> Mrs Miggins.

Betty is <u>less</u> smelly <u>than</u> Mrs Miggins.

Betty is <u>as</u> tall <u>as</u> Mrs Miggins.

Make sure you don't forget the '<u>as</u>' here — and the '<u>than</u>'s above.

> Never write 'more' and '-er' together — it's totally wrong, and you'll be throwing away easy marks. Phrases like 'more better' are just wrong — so don't use them.

Learn these Four Dead Important Comparing Words

These four comparing words <u>don't</u> follow the same rules — so you've got to <u>learn</u> them...

Comparing Words

good/well ➡ better
bad/badly ➡ worse
much ➡ more
little ➡ less

My sister is <u>better</u> at football <u>than</u> my brother.

Melanie had <u>less</u> hair <u>than</u> her Gran.

It just goes from bad to worse...

It'll do your <u>marks</u> no end of good to beef up your writing with some groovy <u>comparisons</u>.
But <u>watch out</u>... if you've written "<u>more</u>" with an "<u>-er</u>" word, those <u>alarm bells</u> should be ringing.

The Best, the Worst and the Least

Sometimes you'll need to write sentences about who or what is the <u>best</u>. Sounds easy enough, but there are a few <u>little tricks</u> to watch out for. Make sure you <u>learn</u> this page carefully.

Writing about the Most — add -est to Short Words

Sometimes using '<u>-er than</u>' or '<u>more</u>' isn't enough — you want to say that something is the <u>best</u> or <u>worst</u>, or the '<u>most</u>' something. For short words, you can usually do this by adding '<u>-est</u>'.

> He had the light<u>est</u> pack in town.

> It was the sharp<u>est</u> pin Leon had ever sat on.

Use 'most' or 'least' for Longer Words

For <u>longer</u> words, it doesn't sound right if you add '<u>-est</u>'. The thing to do here is to use the words '<u>most</u>' and '<u>least</u>', like here:

> He was the <u>least</u> welcome guest at my party.

> She was the <u>most</u> exciting teacher in the world.

OK, it's the best / worst* page... *(delete as appropriate)

It all starts to get a bit fiddly here. Sort out when to use "<u>most</u>" and when to use "<u>-est</u>" — and <u>never</u> use both at the same time. Once you've got to grips with that you're well away...

CLAUSES AND PHRASES

Clauses

Phrases and clauses look a bit confusing at first, but they're just groups of words. A phrase or a clause is part of a sentence and makes it more descriptive.

Sentences are Made up of Clauses

A clause is a bit of a sentence with a verb.

Kaye wrestles sea monsters.

This is a clause — the verb is 'wrestles'. It's also a simple sentence — a sentence with only one clause.

A phrase is a bit of a sentence without a verb.

Kaye wrestles sea monsters in the bath.

This is a phrase. It doesn't contain a verb. It adds extra information to the sentence.

Compound Sentences are made from Equal Clauses

Compound sentences are made of two equally important clauses joined together by a conjunction (a joining word). Each clause would make sense on its own.

Conjunctions are words like 'and', 'or', 'but' or 'because'. See p.22 for more information.

Kaye went to the diving shop.   She bought some flippers.

You can stick these two sentences together with a conjunction like 'and' and bingo — you've got yourself a compound sentence.

I thought I was the most important Clause...

Kaye went to the diving shop and she bought some flippers.

The two clauses in this sentence are just as important as each other.

Clauses

Hold on to your hats, here's some more really useful information about <u>clauses</u> and <u>sentences</u>. It's exciting stuff I know...

Complex Sentences are Built Around a Main Clause

<u>Complex sentences</u> are made up of an <u>important clause</u> and some <u>less important clauses</u>.

The <u>most important clause</u> is called the <u>main clause</u> — it's the <u>main idea</u> of the sentence.

Clare painted the house, while Dave cooked her dinner.

The <u>less important clause</u> in a sentence is called the <u>subordinate clause</u> (or the <u>dependent clause</u>) — it <u>adds extra information</u> to the sentence.

Sometimes the <u>subordinate clause</u> comes <u>first</u>. ➝ *While Dave cooked her dinner, Clare painted the house.*

It's Easy to Spot a Subordinate Clause

1) <u>Main</u> clauses <u>make sense</u> on their <u>own</u>.
2) <u>Subordinate</u> clauses <u>don't make sense</u> on their <u>own</u>.

Laura was late for work because the grasshoppers were protesting.

The <u>main clause</u> <u>makes sense</u> on its own.

The <u>subordinate clause</u> <u>doesn't make sense</u> on its own.

Laura was late for work.

Because the grasshoppers were protesting.

Clause-spotting — it's a great hobby...

You need to make sure you can spot both <u>types of clause</u> — just remember that any clause will include a <u>verb</u> and that a subordinate clause won't make sense on its own and you'll be sorted.

Conjunctions

Your writing will sound a lot <u>better</u> if you use a mixture of <u>long</u> and <u>short</u> sentences. Luckily, there are some cunning ways of putting <u>short</u> sentences <u>together</u> to make <u>longer</u> ones.

Some Conjunctions Join Sentences Together

<u>Compound sentences</u> are made from two sentences. Adding a <u>conjunction</u> like '<u>and</u>', '<u>but</u>' or '<u>so</u>' joins the two clauses together.

Conjunctions can also be called *connectives*.

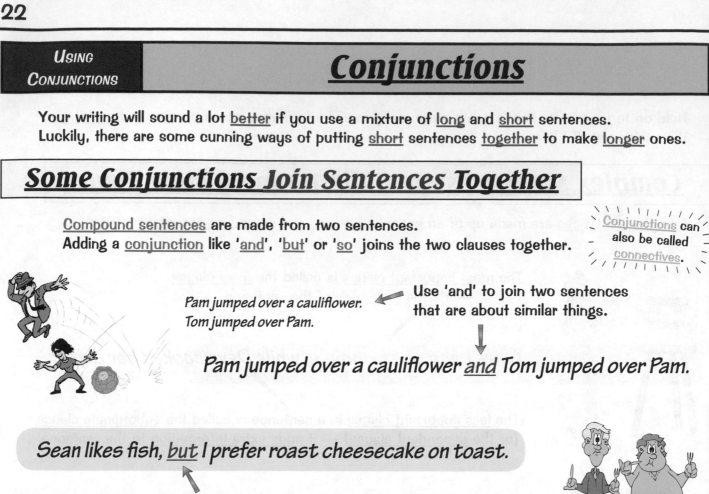

Pam jumped over a cauliflower.
Tom jumped over Pam.

Use 'and' to join two sentences that are about similar things.

Pam jumped over a cauliflower <u>and</u> Tom jumped over Pam.

Sean likes fish, <u>but</u> I prefer roast cheesecake on toast.

By using '<u>but</u>', you're pointing out the <u>difference</u> between the two sentences.

Other Conjunctions are used in Complex Sentences

<u>Complex sentences</u> are made from a <u>main clause</u> and a <u>subordinate clause</u> (see p.21). Words like '<u>while</u>', '<u>before</u>' or '<u>unless</u>' join the two clauses together and show how they are <u>related</u>.

Matilda ate all of the cake <u>before</u> Bruce arrived.

Matilda ate all of the cake.
Bruce arrived.

The conjunction '<u>before</u>' tells you when Matilda ate the cake in relation to Bruce arriving.

Tim refused to play football <u>unless</u> it was snowing.

The conjunction '<u>unless</u>' tells you how the fact that it was snowing is related to Tim playing football.

No excuses — and no buts...

You can join sentences with <u>lots of</u> different <u>conjunctions</u>. Be warned though — the <u>meaning</u> of your sentence will be slightly <u>different</u> — so you'll have to choose which one's <u>best</u> to use.

Paragraphs Make Things Clear

Paragraphs. These jokers are a bit tricky, but that's life. You <u>have to use</u> them, there's no way out, so you'd best learn to love them... or maybe just learn to <u>use them</u> instead.

Paragraphs make your Writing Better

> Paragraphs are dead <u>important</u>.
> Use them and your writing will be bags <u>clearer</u>.

Blimey, we ain't half sinking quickly

TITANIC

Make sure you <u>use</u> paragraphs all the time. If you forget to use them your <u>marks</u> will sink faster than the Titanic. Best get into the habit now so you don't forget.

All the Sentences in a Paragraph are Related

> Paragraphs are groups of sentences which <u>go together</u> — because they talk about the <u>same thing</u>, or because they <u>follow on</u> from each other.

All of the <u>ideas</u> in this paragraph are <u>related</u>. They're all about Henry waking up and listening to see if he can work out what made the crash.

<u>Leave a space</u> at the <u>start</u> of the <u>first line</u> of <u>each paragraph</u>. The <u>space</u> should be about the <u>width</u> of your <u>finger</u>.

...in the light of the full moon.
   There was a crash and Henry sat up in bed. He listened carefully, but the whole house was quiet. Nothing stirred in the darkness, and as Henry listened, he could hear his own heart pounding.
   Downstairs, the monster started to...

<u>Ending a paragraph</u> is <u>easy</u>. Just <u>finish the last sentence</u> of the paragraph and give it a <u>full stop</u>.

Related sentences — those two are cousins...

Paragraphs aren't <u>too</u> hard. Not as hard as mountain-top brain surgery anyway. Just start a <u>new paragraph</u> for each <u>brand new idea</u>, and stick a <u>space</u> at the <u>beginning</u> of the first line.

When to Start a New Paragraph

<u>When</u> to finish one paragraph and start a new one is a <u>tricky</u> business. It's not always obvious, so you need to <u>learn the rules</u> and use your noddle. Start with the golden rule right now.

Start a New Paragraph when Something Changes

This is the <u>golden rule</u> for paragraphs — so you'd better learn it now.

> When you write a story or a letter, you should start a <u>new</u> <u>paragraph</u> every time something <u>changes</u> in the story.

There are <u>five</u> things that could change:

1) When Something New happens

> Whenever you talk about <u>something new</u> happening, you have to use a <u>new paragraph</u>.

This shows that what happens is <u>different</u> from what happened before.

These sentences are about Harry and Sam waiting and being bored, so they're in the same paragraph.

Harry and Sam had been waiting for ages. There was nothing to do, and there was nothing to look at. They were bored.

The buzzing is a new thing, so use a new paragraph.

Suddenly they heard the buzzing. It started off so quietly they could hardly hear it, but it grew and got louder until it rang in their ears like a bell.

The bees are a new thing, so use a new paragraph.

Then they saw the bees — huge, fierce things flying towards them like massive bullets. There were hundreds of them, all in a big swarm.

All new paragraphs — still in the wrapping...

There's just one thing to remember here, but it's dead <u>important</u> — each time <u>something new</u> happens, you must always start a <u>new paragraph</u>. It's easy to forget, but you'll <u>lose marks</u> if you do.

New People and People Speaking

Yup, you've got it — two more really <u>important</u> cases to <u>learn</u>. When you write a story or letter, use a <u>new paragraph</u> every time you write about a <u>new person</u> and every time a person actually <u>speaks</u>.

2) When you Talk about a New Person

Whenever a <u>new person</u> appears in your writing, you should start a <u>new paragraph</u> — it shows the reader that something has <u>changed</u>.

Up, up and away!

New paragraph to talk about Naomi.

Ryan swung his racket and smacked the ball up into the air. It flew up into the sky and then fell like a stone onto Naomi's head.

Naomi was normally a quiet, friendly girl. She had been watching the tennis match for five minutes or so, without saying anything. When the ball hit her, though, she burst into tears.

3) Each time a Person Speaks

When you write a story, it's important to put in some sentences where the people involved actually <u>say or think</u> something.

Every time someone <u>starts speaking</u>, you start a <u>new paragraph</u>.

That includes when one person stops talking, and someone else starts.

Alison is actually speaking so start a new paragraph.

When the same person keeps on talking, you don't have to start a new paragraph.

Here the speaker has changed so you start a new paragraph.

The fisherman was sitting in his boat when Alison came to the end of the jetty.

"Have you caught anything?" she asked.

"I haven't caught a thing all day," growled the fisherman crossly. He was busy mending his nets.

"Better luck tomorrow!" replied Alison. "You never know what you might catch then. Maybe a shark!"

"There aren't any sharks around here," said the fisherman.

"What's that then?" asked Alison, pointing to the big blue fin in the water.

New people? — I don't like strangers...

<u>Two more</u> times when you have to start a <u>new paragraph</u> here then. This needs to find itself a home between your ears — if you wrote that fisherman story as <u>one big lump</u> it'd be dang <u>hard</u> to read.

NEW PLACES AND TIMES	# When the Place or Time Changes

When you write about a <u>new place</u> or a <u>new time</u>, you have to start a <u>new paragraph</u>.
If what you're talking about <u>moves</u> from Brighton Pier to Bangalore, then that's a <u>new paragraph</u>, pal.

4) *When you Write about a Different Place*

> Every time the story or letter moves to <u>another place</u>, you need to start a <u>new paragraph</u>.

This helps the reader to see that you're writing about <u>something different</u>.

This paragraph is about the jungle.

The elephants were stampeding through the jungle. They knocked down trees left and right, and all the other animals were running for their lives.
Back in the village, Adele was doing her homework when the ground began to shake.

This is about the village = new paragraph.

5) *When the Story or Letter Moves to a Different Time*

Sometimes a story or a letter <u>moves in time</u>. It can go backwards or forwards to talk about something that happened at a <u>different time</u>.

> Whenever the story or letter <u>moves in time</u>, you should start a <u>new paragraph</u>.

Today I went to school, and it was a boring day. It was raining at break time so we weren't allowed outside.
Yesterday it was really sunny, though. The weather was so nice we went outside to do a class experiment in the wild area.

Each paragraph talks about a different time.

This has gone forward to a different time.

It was late so we decided to go home.
The next day we got up early. We wanted to see if we could catch the goblins dancing in the forest before dawn.

Revise paragraphs — this is the time and the place...

So, the <u>five times</u> when you have to use paragraphs are when — 1) <u>something new</u> happens, 2) you talk about a <u>new person</u>, 3) someone <u>speaks</u>, 4) you write about a <u>different place</u>, or 5) you move to a <u>different time</u>. It's all about breaking your writing into <u>chunks</u>, so that people can understand what you're going on about. Learn 'em, <u>use</u> 'em, and wriggle with joy.

Plan it Before You Write it

COMING UP WITH A PLOT

This is earth-shatteringly <u>important</u>, so sit up and take notice. <u>Before</u> you rush headlong into your story, you need to <u>make a plan</u> of what is going to happen. <u>Think</u> first, get <u>marks</u>, grin later.

Decide Who, What and Where

If you're writing a story there are <u>three</u> main things to do to <u>plan</u> your story.

Planning a Story

1) Decide <u>what</u> is going to <u>happen</u>.
2) Work out <u>who</u> is <u>involved</u> in the events.
3) Choose <u>where</u> it will all happen.

When you're making your plan, you don't need to write in full sentences.

A story needs to have <u>action</u> and something needs to <u>happen</u> for it to be interesting. Imagine a story where <u>nothing happened</u>. That'd be as boring as doing your 13 times table up to 13 times 17 462 758.

A story has a Beginning, a Middle and an End

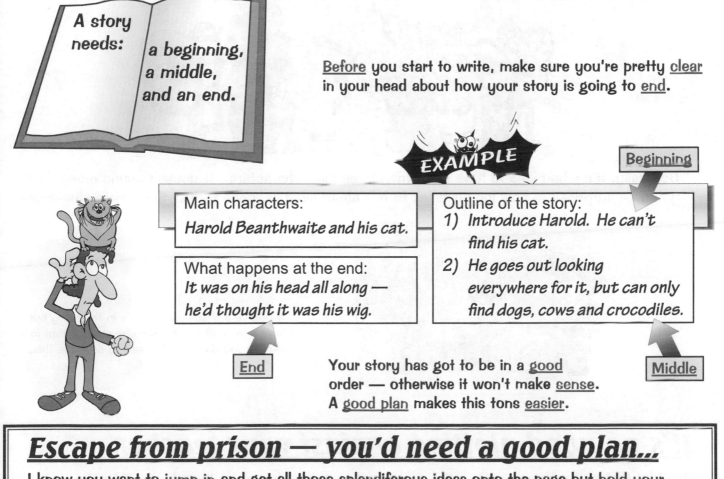

A story needs: a beginning, a middle, and an end.

<u>Before</u> you start to write, make sure you're pretty <u>clear</u> in your head about how your story is going to <u>end</u>.

EXAMPLE

Main characters:
Harold Beanthwaite and his cat.

What happens at the end:
It was on his head all along — he'd thought it was his wig.

Outline of the story:
1) *Introduce Harold. He can't find his cat.*
2) *He goes out looking everywhere for it, but can only find dogs, cows and crocodiles.*

Beginning

End

Middle

Your story has got to be in a <u>good</u> order — otherwise it won't make <u>sense</u>. A <u>good plan</u> makes this tons <u>easier</u>.

Escape from prison — you'd need a good plan...

I know you want to <u>jump in</u> and get all those splendiferous ideas onto the page but <u>hold your horses</u>. Make a <u>plan</u> first or you could end up in a right <u>muddle</u>. You know I'm right, admit it.

| ACHIEVABLE GOALS | # Don't Try to Write Too Much |

You won't have bags of time to write your story. <u>Don't</u> make it too <u>long</u>, or it'll all come unstuck.

Don't write Too Much Plot

Whatever you do, <u>don't</u> let your plan get <u>too long</u>.

If your plan is too long, you might <u>not have time</u> to finish writing the story. Then you'll have to rush at the end, and you'll end up with a right mess. Just write about a <u>few</u> things.

Don't have Too Many Characters

Don't have <u>too many people</u> in your story. If you describe loads of them then you won't have space for any <u>actual story</u>, and that would be a complete disaster.

Generally, it's a <u>bad idea</u> to have more than <u>three</u> main characters. It doesn't sound many, but you'd be surprised at how long it takes to talk about what happens to just three main characters.

If you've got someone who's in the story but isn't a main character (maybe an assistant in a shop), you don't really need to describe them.

It's no good plotting against your teacher...

Don't let that plot <u>run away</u> with you — you won't have time to write a <u>huge book</u>. Trim it down so you can write it <u>well</u> in the time you're given — then you won't have to <u>rush</u> and leave it <u>half-baked</u>.

How to Start Your Story

The <u>beginning</u> of a story is <u>mega-important</u>. No-one wants to read a story with a <u>boring</u> start — your reader needs to be <u>hooked</u> from the very first line. Learn these two secrets of <u>success</u>.

Two Great ways to Begin

The beginning needs to **grab** the reader's **attention**.

LISTEN TO ME!

Not the best way to grab attention.

A <u>good beginning</u> makes the reader want to keep reading — they'll think the rest of the story will be good, too.

1) Start in the Middle of a Dramatic Event

Start with something <u>exciting</u>, and the person reading your story can't help but want to <u>read on</u>. They'll want to find out what happens next.

Example

Sarah shut her eyes as the ground shook around her. An earthquake!

2) Start with a Character Speaking

If you start with someone <u>speaking</u>, the person reading your story will want to find out <u>who</u> they are and <u>what</u> they're talking about.

EXAMPLE

"Be careful with those marshmallows!" shouted John, but it was no use. Tim had decided that he was going to take his marshmallows to the moon, and there was no stopping him.

The first line of your story can tell you about what is <u>happening</u>. Don't explain <u>everything</u> at once. Make the reader <u>want</u> to read on.

Get a good start — have a hearty breakfast...

Trust me on this — you need to grab your reader's <u>attention</u> and make them want to <u>read on</u>. Think of interesting, gripping <u>starts</u> that will stop even the sleepiest reader from nodding off.

WRITING IN THE 1ST & 3RD PERSON

Who's Telling the Story

This is about whether or not <u>you</u> are in the story. The important thing is to <u>decide</u> which you're doing at the start and <u>not</u> to <u>switch</u> from one to the other... got it? Good.

If You are a Character in the story write as 'I'

Write about the things that <u>you</u> see and hear and feel in the story, <u>not</u> stuff other people saw but you wouldn't have known about.

I was in the kitchen eating some toast when it happened. I couldn't believe my eyes.

Never write about Other Characters using 'I'

Writing about the <u>main character</u> as 'he' or 'she' can be tricky. If you're given a first line that talks about the main character as '<u>he</u>' or '<u>she</u>', then you must <u>stick with it</u>.

If you start by talking about your main character as 'he' or 'she', don't start talking about them as 'I' — even if they're just like you.

Example

Bill was hanging inches from shark infested water, and he was praying for his life.

Meanwhile, the Masked Avenger was speeding up the river in his powerboat, on his way to rescue me from the sharks.

Argh. This starts off talking about Bill, and then talks about him as "me".

> Basically, you're either <u>in</u> the story
> or you're <u>not</u>. <u>Don't</u> get it mixed up.

Make Sure it's Clear Who 'He' is

When you use '<u>he</u>' and '<u>she</u>' to write about your main characters, <u>watch out</u>.

Example

Meanwhile, the Masked Avenger was speeding up the river in his powerboat, on his way to Bill's rescue. He saw him and called out to him.

Don't let this happen — you can't tell whether Bill saw the Masked Avenger, or the Masked Avenger saw Bill.

My own point of view — from the window...

Once you've made a choice <u>stick with it</u> — if you aren't a character in the story, don't start writing as 'I'. Don't let yourself forget halfway through, or your story will be a right muddle.

Stick to 'It was...' or 'It is...'

If you're writing about something that happened in the <u>past</u>, write that way <u>all</u> the way through your story. <u>Don't</u> chop and change between '<u>is</u>' and '<u>was</u>' — it'll make your story a <u>mess</u>.

It's got to Make Sense

A Crucial Point

If you start off writing about things as if they happened in the <u>past</u>, <u>don't change</u> and start writing as if things are happening <u>as you write</u>.

So if you're using 'I was', 'they were', 'they went' and so on, don't suddenly <u>change</u> to 'I am', 'they are' and 'they go'. It'd make your story <u>confusing and difficult</u> to read — and that means goodbye to loads of <u>precious marks</u>.

Joel and Emma opened the door very slowly and peered into the barn. It was dark, so they couldn't see anything except a few bales of straw.
Suddenly, they heard a rustling sound. Emma is terrified and just manages not to scream. Joel hid behind the door. "What was that?" he whispers.

This should be 'managed'.

This should be 'was'.

This should be 'whispered'.

Joel and Emma were terrified, but it was only a chicken.

When this starts talking about things as if they're happening <u>at the moment</u>, it doesn't make sense. That's a bad thing.

Keep it the Same as the First sentence

Sometimes you'll be given the <u>first</u> sentence of a story, and you have to finish it off. If that happens, then keep it the <u>same</u>. If it starts by talking as if it's something that happened in the <u>past</u>, don't write as if it's <u>happening now</u>. It's no big deal to remember that — so make sure you do.

Writing in the past — scrolls and quills...

Wave bye-bye to lots of <u>easy marks</u> if you don't get this right. It's a <u>common mistake</u> to swap between 'it is' and 'it was' and 'we are' and 'we were'. Just make sure you <u>don't</u> do it. Alrighty!

Describing Things Well

A cool trick in story writing is to use big fancy glorious, gob-stopping describing <u>words</u>. Use them all over the place — for <u>what</u> happens, <u>where</u> it happens, <u>who's</u> there and what everything's <u>like</u>.

Describe Things and People in the story

When someone is reading a story, they need to know what's <u>going on</u>.
You need to tell them <u>two</u> things so they can <u>understand</u> your stories.

Describe the <u>people</u> in the story.

Describe what <u>happens</u>.

Your characters will <u>only</u> be good if you <u>describe</u> them — else no-one reading the story will know what they're meant to be like.

It wouldn't be much fun if you were reading a story and didn't know what was <u>happening</u>. So make sure that people reading yours <u>do</u> know.

Tell them about me!

Tell them about ME!

Three Great Ways to use Describing Words

Describing words are <u>very cool</u>. Use them in <u>all</u> your stories.

These describe the caterpillar.

EXAMPLE

<u>Adjectives</u> can tell you about the <u>people</u> or <u>things</u> in the sentence.

If you need to remind yourself about adjectives have a look at p.4.

I was face to face with a giant, hairy, orange caterpillar.

Tom sang loudly.

Example

To jog your memory on adverbs take a peek at p.6.

<u>Adverbs</u> can tell you more about the <u>action</u> in a sentence.
They tell you <u>how</u> something was done.

Describing words can bring the story to life. They tell you how the characters were <u>feeling</u>, and what the <u>mood</u> of a scene was like.

Example

The cold sea air made Andrew cough. Miserable, he shivered in his wet T-shirt.

A clearer picture — where are my specs...

To write a great <u>story</u>, one thing you've really got to do is put in <u>dead good descriptions</u> of things. Your story'll be a lot more <u>interesting</u> — and it'll get you lots more juicy <u>marks</u>.

Three Cool Types of Image

SIMILES, METAPHORS AND ONOMATOPOEIA

An image is just a fancy way of saying <u>what</u> something is <u>like</u>. Use them to make your story loads more <u>interesting</u>, and to give the reader a really good <u>picture</u> in their mind of what's <u>going on</u>.

1) *Things are Like each other*

You can say one thing is <u>like</u> another — comparing them.

Max's shadow was huge and menacing, <u>like Frankenstein's monster</u>.

This is called a simile.

2) *Something Is Something else*

You can say one thing <u>is</u> another — when you mean it's <u>like</u> the other thing.

Shakespeare was a <u>lumbering bear</u> on the dance floor.

This is called a metaphor.

This doesn't mean that Shakespeare turned into a bear every time he went out for a boogie. It means he danced like a bear.

3) *Something Sounds Like what it's Talking about*

Some words <u>sound</u> a bit like what they're talking about:

This is called onomatopoeia.

<u>'Creak'</u> went the stairs as Shakespeare climbed up them.

<u>Crash</u>! The door <u>smashed</u> apart as Max walked through it.

Get a new image — dye your hair green...

Describe the things in your stories in the most <u>interesting</u> way you can. Come up with some <u>juicy</u> ways of saying what something's <u>like</u>, and your <u>marks</u> will go up quicker than a factory full of fireworks. It doesn't have to be earth-shattering, as long as it's <u>not</u> bog standard.

Writing Speech

Unless you want to write 'The Most Boring Story in the World... Ever' your characters need to <u>speak</u> and <u>think</u>. Read on to learn how to write <u>speech</u> properly.

Speech can Tell You what's Happening

"Look," said Alison, "here's an old wooden trunk."

My trunk's not old.

This tells you that Alison has found a wooden trunk.

You <u>don't</u> need to write 'Alison found an old trunk' after this, because it's pretty obvious from what she's said.

There's nothing to be scared about silly

"Don't go to the park, Sally!" said Eric.
"They'll be waiting for you."

This tells you Sally was going to go to the park, but Eric is warning her not to.

Speech can Show what a Character is Like

1) You can give people an idea of what someone is like by <u>what</u> they say.

It's easy enough. Just <u>think</u> about what kind of person each character is, and what that kind of person would <u>say</u>.

Example "I'm the best!" announced the boxer. "No one else comes close!"

This shows that the character is confident, and has a really high opinion of himself.

2) You can get people to see what a character is like by <u>how</u> they say things.

Example "I would be quite delighted if you would be so kind as to accept my invitation to dine with me this evening," Adrian declared.

This shows that Adrian is a bit posh, but Annie is down-to-earth and casual.

"You can grab a bit of grub 'round my place if you like," suggested Annie.

Speech — get a word in edgeways...

Pep up your <u>story</u> with some juicy speech. It's a brilliant way to show what people are <u>like</u>, and to keep your story moving. Remember the <u>speech marks</u> when someone's speaking (see p.14-15).

Using the Same Old Words is Boring

<u>Stop</u> your stories being boring as mud by <u>using</u> some of these top ways of <u>saying</u> what you <u>mean</u>.

Nothing is Ever just 'Nice'

If you ever say that something is <u>nice</u>, you can bet that you could be a <u>lot</u> more <u>interesting</u> if you use a different word or phrase.

The film was...

| exciting | brilliant | scary, but I felt sorry for the villain at the end... |

These biscuits are...

| crunchy like sand | perfect with coffee |
| melt-in-the-mouth gorgeous | delicious |

Scrumbo Bickies
Better Than Your Nana's Ginger Biscuits!

Don't use the Same words Over and Over again

Example

Craig looked out to <u>sea</u>. He walked to the edge of the <u>sea</u> and dipped his toes in the <u>sea</u>.

With 'sea' repeated like this it's boring.

Craig looked out to sea. He walked down to the shore and dipped his toes in the water.

This is stacks better.

Try using Different words for 'Said'

Using 'he <u>said</u>...', 'she <u>said</u>...', 'then he <u>said</u>...' all the time will make your story dead <u>boring</u>. You can use lots of <u>different</u> verbs to show how someone is <u>speaking</u>, but they all have a different meaning. Here are some examples to get you started...

"Where is my money?" <u>demanded</u> Mr Wilson.

<u>Demanded</u> is a good word to use for a really forceful question.

"You'll get your money at the end of the week," <u>replied</u> the assistant calmly.

Use <u>replied</u> or <u>answered</u> when someone answers.

"Fractions. Don't talk to me about fractions," <u>muttered</u> Simon.

<u>Muttered</u> lets you know Simon was speaking very quietly.

Don't repeat yourself — ever...ever...ever...ever...

There are oodles of <u>different</u> ways you could say things. The secret is to <u>keep learning new words</u>. Keep your <u>eyes peeled</u> whenever you <u>read</u> anything — if you see a word that you don't understand <u>find out</u> what it means. Remember, <u>boring</u> writing means measly <u>marks</u>.

Stick With the Same Style

Give your story buckets of <u>personality</u> and you'll get loads more marks — simple.

Use words that Fit with the Feeling of your story

If you want your story to be <u>happy</u>, then use bags of <u>happy</u> sounding words. If it's going to be a <u>sad</u> story, stick in loads of <u>sad</u> words. If it's a <u>funny</u> story, use <u>funny</u> words. How easy is that?

You have to use descriptions that fit the feeling of the story, too. If it's a really <u>happy</u> story, describing everything as <u>dark</u>, <u>scary</u> and <u>miserable</u> isn't the best idea in the world.

It was a dark scary night and Carrie and Cuthbert were feeling miserable.

Choose if it's Realistic or not — and Stick with it

Sometimes your story will be the kind of thing that could <u>really happen</u>.
Sometimes you'll write a story about things that would <u>never happen</u>. That's OK,
loads of films about space and aliens and monsters or whatever aren't possible, either.

Make sure you know if your story is going to be <u>realistic</u> or not — <u>decide</u> when you make your <u>plan</u>.

Stick with it.

Or else.

If you start off writing a <u>realistic</u> story, don't have aliens walking in the front door without thinking <u>very</u> carefully about it.

I'm <u>not</u> giving it up!

One more thing. If your story is unrealistic, don't <u>go overboard</u>. So if your story's about sea monsters in the ocean, then it's <u>not</u> a smart move to suddenly go off to the moon, get attacked by aliens and meet your favourite band on Mars.

Generally, <u>one</u> unrealistic thing is enough.

Make people cry — without chopping onions...

Decide what you want your story to be <u>like</u> — then use the <u>right</u> kind of words and descriptions to <u>make</u> it that way. A story which is jam-packed with colourful words will <u>grab</u> more juicy <u>marks</u>.

Writing a Good Ending

It's seriously <u>important</u> this — a really rubbish ending can totally <u>ruin</u> a good story. Writing endings can be <u>tough</u>. The only way to make it <u>easier</u> and improve your <u>marks</u>, is to <u>learn</u> how.

Don't just Stop

Plan your ending first.
It's the only way.

Whatever you do, don't just <u>stop</u> and write '<u>The End</u>'. Your ending has to tie up all the loose ends.

The <u>only</u> way to write a great ending is to <u>plan</u> it out first, <u>before</u> you start writing.

It's <u>no good</u> just leaving it all to chance and hoping you think of something <u>brilliant</u> at the last minute. That's just plain <u>daft</u>.

Don't say it was all a Dream

OK, here you just have to <u>trust</u> me. Whatever you do, <u>do not</u> break this golden rule.

The Golden Rule of Endings

<u>Never</u> finish with 'I woke up and it had all been a dream.'

It's about the <u>worst</u> ending you could ever imagine and it's been done millions of times before. Using it is a guaranteed way to <u>lose marks</u>. Just <u>don't</u> ever, ever even think of using it. Not even a tiny bit.

Read Back Over your story

When you've written a story, read <u>every</u> paragraph to check it's <u>easy</u> to see what's going on — make sure that someone reading the story for the <u>first time</u> would <u>understand</u> it.

My fish does not open all spanners.

Of course it's clear, I understand it.

1) Check it's <u>clear</u> what happens in your story.

2) Make sure it's clear <u>who</u> the people are and <u>what</u> they're like.

3) If it's not clear you'd best go back and change it...

A dog with two tails — what a weird ending...

If there's one thing that'll make the person reading your story <u>wince</u>, it's a <u>naff</u> and <u>nasty</u> ending. Coming up with a good one can be pretty <u>tricky</u> though. To get the hang of it, <u>have a go</u> at thinking up brilliant endings to stories — and remember, don't <u>ever</u> say "it was all a dream"...

WRITING FORMAL LETTERS

Writing a Formal Letter

You may be given a chance to <u>write a letter</u>, either a <u>formal</u> or an <u>informal</u> one.
<u>Formal letters</u> follow a strict set of <u>rules</u>, which are shown in <u>blue</u> in the letter below.
Look at the letter and <u>learn the rules</u> for writing them:

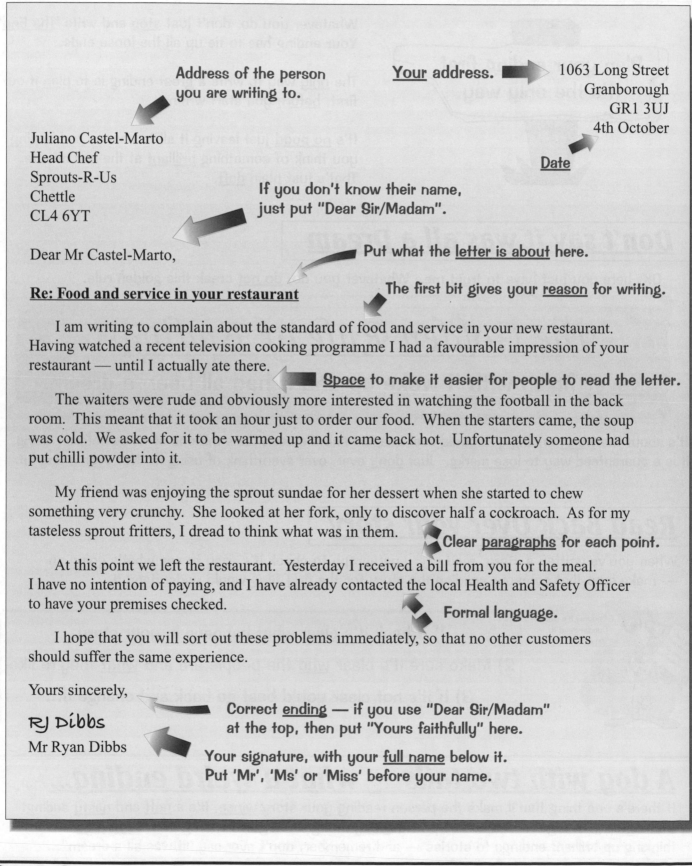

Address of the person you are writing to.

<u>Your</u> address. ➡ 1063 Long Street
Granborough
GR1 3UJ
4th October

Date

Juliano Castel-Marto
Head Chef
Sprouts-R-Us
Chettle
CL4 6YT

If you don't know their name, just put "Dear Sir/Madam".

Dear Mr Castel-Marto,

Put what the <u>letter is about</u> here.

<u>Re: Food and service in your restaurant</u>

The first bit gives your <u>reason</u> for writing.

    I am writing to complain about the standard of food and service in your new restaurant. Having watched a recent television cooking programme I had a favourable impression of your restaurant — until I actually ate there.

<u>Space</u> to make it easier for people to read the letter.

    The waiters were rude and obviously more interested in watching the football in the back room. This meant that it took an hour just to order our food. When the starters came, the soup was cold. We asked for it to be warmed up and it came back hot. Unfortunately someone had put chilli powder into it.

    My friend was enjoying the sprout sundae for her dessert when she started to chew something very crunchy. She looked at her fork, only to discover half a cockroach. As for my tasteless sprout fritters, I dread to think what was in them.

Clear <u>paragraphs</u> for each point.

    At this point we left the restaurant. Yesterday I received a bill from you for the meal. I have no intention of paying, and I have already contacted the local Health and Safety Officer to have your premises checked.

Formal language.

    I hope that you will sort out these problems immediately, so that no other customers should suffer the same experience.

Yours sincerely,

Correct <u>ending</u> — if you use "Dear Sir/Madam" at the top, then put "Yours faithfully" here.

RJ Dibbs
Mr Ryan Dibbs

Your signature, with your <u>full name</u> below it.
Put 'Mr', 'Ms' or 'Miss' before your name.

Using Formal Language

So <u>formal letters</u> have to look right — but that's not all. If you want to pick up some juicy <u>marks</u>, you'd better use the right <u>sort</u> of words. Read on and all will be revealed...

Use Formal Language in a Formal Letter

When you write a <u>formal letter</u>, you don't only have to make sure it <u>looks</u> right. You have to use the right type of <u>language</u> as well. Formal language can be a bit tricky.

Formal language is the sort that's used in the letters you take home from school. It often <u>doesn't</u> sound like it's talking <u>directly</u> to someone. It says what <u>should happen</u> and what <u>needs to be done</u> instead of telling you directly to do something. It also often uses longer words...

(1) Instead of writing *'I got'* ✗
   write *'I <u>received</u>'*. ✓

Look Miss, I've written a letter.

(2) Instead of writing *'We want you to...'* ✗
   write *'It is <u>expected</u> that you will...'* ✓

(3) Instead of writing *'Please write to or phone Mr Smith'* ✗
   write *'Please <u>contact</u> Mr Smith.'* ✓

(4) Instead of writing *'When you're in the museum, you must be quiet'* ✗
   write *'Visitors are <u>requested</u> to remain silent'*. ✓

(5) Also, don't use shortened words like *'can't'*, *'won't'* and *'TV'*. ✗
   Write them out in full as *'<u>cannot</u>'*, *'<u>will not</u>'* and *'<u>television</u>'*. ✓

Don't use Exclamation Marks

Formal language <u>doesn't</u> use <u>exclamation marks</u>. You can write polite questions — remember that these need question marks. Make sure that your <u>questions</u> are <u>polite</u>.

What! No exclamation marks!

Remember — formal language is what's used in the letters that you get from <u>school</u> (well, most of them anyway). Look at loads of them, and <u>compare</u> them to the stuff on this page. The more you look at, the more the facts will lodge themselves in your brain. Soon it will all seem so <u>easy</u>...

Writing an Informal Letter

If you're writing to a <u>friend</u> or someone else you <u>know very well</u>, then you can write an <u>informal</u> <u>letter</u>. Informal letters are much more <u>friendly</u>, and you <u>don't</u> have to bother with all the fancy formal language like on the last page. Take a look at this letter...

Give your <u>address</u>
(it makes it easier for the other person to reply).

54 Derby Road
Littlewitch
LW4 6RT
15th July

<u>First</u> name, because you're writing to a <u>friend</u>.

Dear Tony,

Chatty, friendly style.

Thanks for writing back so soon. It sounds like you had an awesome time in France, but you'll never believe what happened to us!

<u>Exclamation</u> mark.

You remember we were supposed to be going to Ibiza? Well, we had everything ready the night before and we got up really early to go to the airport. All of us were dead tired, especially Mum and Dad, because I was the one who realised we'd left Mandy at home!

<u>Shortened</u> forms of words.

Unbelievable, isn't it! We had to turn around and go right back. Fortunately Mandy had plenty of water, so she was fine. We had been supposed to take her to the "Dog's Life" Kennels first thing, but we were all so tired that we forgot!

Don't forget the <u>spaces</u> to make it easier to read.

It meant we missed our flight, but at least Mandy was OK. Can you imagine what a mess she would have made in the house if we had left her for a week?

Everything turned out fine though. We got a later flight and had an excellent time. It was even better knowing that Mandy was safely at the Kennels.

Must go, but I'll write again soon. Till then,

<u>Paragraphs</u> for each point or different part of the story (it makes the letter easier to read).

Take it easy,

Informal ending.

Steve

Just sign your <u>first</u> name.

Using Chatty Language

These friendly letters should be a <u>doddle</u>... but only if you think them over properly and make sure you use <u>proper sentences</u>. Here's how to write them...

Informal Letters use casual Chatty Language

① Even though you're writing in a <u>friendly</u> way, you must still use <u>proper sentences</u> — or you'll lose absolutely oodles of marks.

② Imagine that you're actually <u>talking</u> to the person you're writing to, and use the same sort of language — it will sound more <u>natural</u>.

③ Look back at the example — it's okay to use shortened words like '<u>don't</u>', '<u>can't</u>' and '<u>isn't</u>' — and <u>exclamation marks</u> !

④ Try looking back to the formal letter, and <u>compare</u> it to the one on the <u>last page</u> to see the <u>differences</u>.

How's it goin' me old matey-bubs?

Informal Lettuce

Whatever the Type of letter — always Plan it...

① <u>Planning</u> a letter is just as important as planning a story. If you <u>don't</u> plan it out first, you won't do the <u>best job</u> that you possibly can.

② Write down the <u>main points</u> that you want to make in the letter. <u>Don't</u> try to say <u>too much</u> in the letter or you won't have <u>time</u> to write it all.

③ If the question gives you ideas and points that you <u>have</u> to include, you must put them <u>all</u> in.

...and get that Layout right

Informal letters still need to have the address in the right place, but you don't need to finish with '<u>Yours sincerely</u>'. Just end with '<u>Lots of love</u>', '<u>See you soon</u>', '<u>Write back soon!</u>', '<u>Cheers, mate</u>' or anything that shows you're writing to someone you know.

Informal Letters — Chatty, chatty, bang, bang...

You'd think it would be easy to be informal, but there's lots of tricky little things to watch out for. The hard bit is making it <u>sound</u> like you're <u>talking</u> to them, but still using <u>proper sentences</u>. If you don't use proper sentences, you'll lose a heap of marks, so really <u>think</u> about what you're writing.

How to Plan a Newsletter

Instead of a letter, you may get the chance to write a <u>newsletter</u>. Never fear — they're not so bad. If you just <u>plan</u> it properly and follow these <u>tips</u>, you'll be well away...

Plan it out First

As with letters, always <u>plan</u> a newsletter before you start to write. A good way to do this is to make a <u>list</u> of <u>everything</u> that needs to go in.

The question will <u>tell</u> you <u>some</u> things to put in, but there's <u>others</u> you'll have to <u>think of</u>. Here's a great way of remembering everything — think of all the <u>'wh' questions</u>...

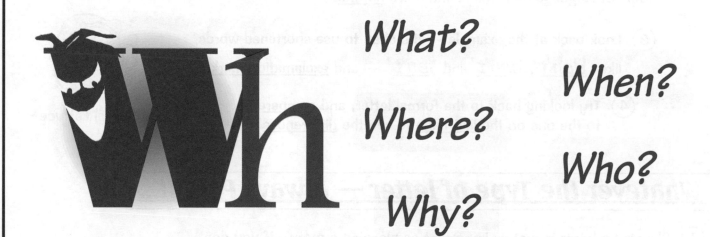

What?

When?

Where?

Who?

Why?

Once you think you've listed <u>everything</u>, just go through these questions in case they <u>remind</u> you of something you've forgotten.

For example, if it's a newsletter about an <u>event</u> that will be happening soon you must say <u>what's</u> happening, <u>when</u> it's happening, <u>where</u> it's happening, <u>who</u> will be there, and <u>why</u> it's happening.

Always Start by saying what the Newsletter is About

This is mind-blowingly important. When someone reads a newsletter, they want to know <u>what it's about</u>, so make sure you say this <u>right at the top</u>.

And <u>remember</u> — if you don't put in things that the question <u>tells</u> you to put in, then you <u>will</u> lose out on marks. The most important thing is to answer the question <u>properly</u>.

How to Write a Newsletter

One of the main things you've got to plan is what you actually <u>say</u>, and <u>how</u> you say it. Ignore these <u>splendid tips</u> at your peril...

Be Careful when you Make Things Up

① Make sure you're <u>allowed</u> to make things up. If you're writing about a <u>made up</u> place, then you must think carefully about what it's <u>like</u> and what people can <u>do</u> there.

② The most important thing is to make it <u>realistic</u>. If it's <u>not</u> very believable, then you're not likely to get too many <u>marks</u> for it.

③ What you write has to make <u>sense</u>. Read it through and make sure that what you're talking about is <u>perfectly clear</u>. The person reading your newsletter has to <u>understand</u> what you're talking about.

Think about what Style to use

① If you're writing a newsletter from <u>school</u> then <u>pretend</u> you're the <u>teacher</u>. Use the kind of <u>words</u> they use and say the kinds of things they <u>say</u>.

Blurg!

② Look at the <u>letters</u> you get sent home from school and write like they do.

③ Remember to use <u>formal language</u> — don't use shortened words like 'didn't' and 'can't'.

Hot News: Shrinking Headline Tragedy. Where Will It End?

Don't panic... all you've got to do is <u>write some stuff</u> on the page and <u>make it look good</u>. OK it's a <u>bit</u> harder than that, but it doesn't have to be a nightmare. A <u>good plan</u> is to work out what you want to say first, and <u>then</u> work out how to lay it out on the page.

Writing Leaflets

<u>Leaflets</u> are a bit like newsletters — but with a lot <u>less writing</u> and <u>more pretty pictures</u>. The difference is they're trying to <u>advertise</u> something — so they must grab your attention.

The Layout is very Important

The thing you really must do is <u>plan</u> your leaflet first. How it <u>looks</u> is really important, so you've got to give it lots of thought <u>before</u> you start.

It's always best to do a <u>rough sketch</u> first, just so that you know where everything's going to go.

Say how Brilliant it is

You need to say <u>why</u> the thing or the place you're advertising is <u>so good</u>. When you plan your leaflet, think of <u>three or four brilliant things</u> about the place or the product and write them down.

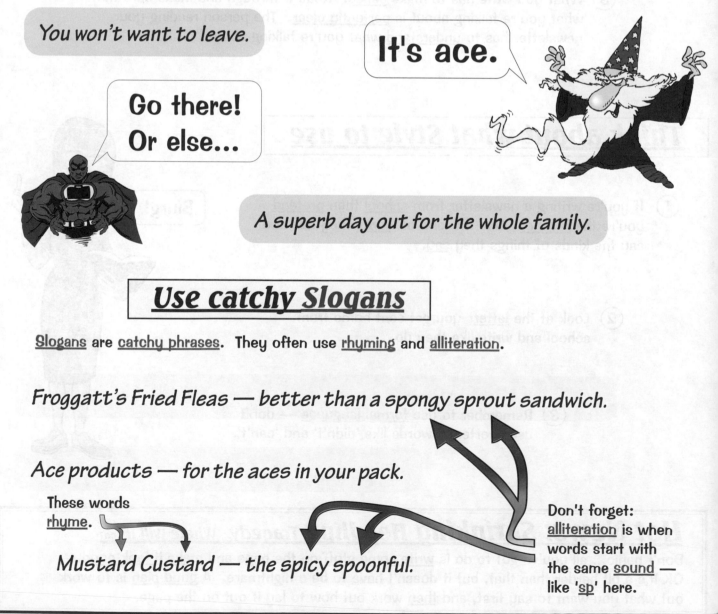

You won't want to leave.

It's ace.

*Go there!
Or else...*

A superb day out for the whole family.

Use catchy Slogans

<u>Slogans</u> are <u>catchy phrases</u>. They often use <u>rhyming</u> and <u>alliteration</u>.

Froggatt's Fried Fleas — better than a spongy sprout sandwich.

Ace products — for the aces in your pack.

These words <u>rhyme</u>.

Mustard Custard — the spicy spoonful.

Don't forget: <u>alliteration</u> is when words start with the same <u>sound</u> — like 'sp' here.

Setting Out Your Leaflets

Working out what you want to say is only <u>half</u> of writing a leaflet. How it <u>looks</u> is really really really important too. <u>Mega</u> important in fact. So think '<u>pictures</u>' and read on...

Pictures make the leaflet Eye-catching

Don't forget to use a <u>picture</u> or two. They really make loads of difference to how it <u>looks</u>.

But be really <u>careful</u> though — <u>don't spend too much time drawing</u>. You won't get a whole load of marks if you don't have time to write anything. The most important thing is to <u>finish it</u>.

Check out this cunning <u>example</u>, then <u>look back</u> at the stuff on the last page to see <u>how</u> it's used...

Work out the most <u>important</u> thing that you're going to say. Give it pride of place at the <u>top</u>.

Posters and leaflets have something big and <u>eye-catching</u> at the <u>top</u> or in the <u>middle</u>. The details are in smaller writing at the bottom.

Use <u>bullet points</u> like these to make things stand out better.

And don't forget those <u>catchy slogans</u>...

Broughton Towers
The day out with a difference

Broughton by night

See Flossybot Parsons, duckling extraordinaire.

There's something for everyone at Broughton...

- *marvel at the wild and wacky tea bag collection*
- *count the sheep in the surrounding hills*
- *buy an organic cucumber from the local shop*
- *find en suite bathrooms you didn't know existed*
- *loads of things for kids to do too*

...So don't delay — visit today.

For further details, why not visit our web site at www.beetroot.co.mars

Eye-catching — it's a big deal for eye jugglers...

Lovely pictures are very important. But whatever you do, don't spend all your time drawing them — you won't have time for your short, sharp, mind-bogglingly <u>fantastic</u> sentences and catchy <u>slogans</u>. Oh yes, and take a good look at any leaflets you come across to see how they're done.

Writing Good Interview Questions

You may have the chance to write an <u>interview</u>. It's a different kettle of fish altogether — it's a <u>conversation</u>. You decide what to <u>ask</u> them. You decide what they <u>say</u>. It's all in your hands...

Ask the Right Questions

Just like any other piece of writing, always <u>plan</u> an interview before you write it. Start by making a short <u>list</u> of the things you want to include.

<u>Imagine</u> you really were interviewing the person. Think of the sort of things you would <u>want</u> to know. Ask them <u>interesting</u> things about their <u>life</u> and <u>what they do</u>.

If you're <u>told</u> to ask a particular question, then make sure you include it in your <u>plan</u> so that you don't forget to ask it.

> *"So, what was the inspiration behind your latest song, 'I hate pickled walnuts'?"*

Don't use Yes/No questions

Remember — an interview is a <u>conversation</u>, so try to make it <u>sound</u> like a conversation.

If the person you're interviewing can answer your questions by just saying "<u>yes</u>" or "<u>no</u>", then it won't be a very <u>interesting</u> conversation. Always write the questions so that they <u>can't</u> just give a "yes" or "no" answer. Take a look at these...

Instead of asking, *"Do you like mashed sprouts?"* ✗

ask, *"What do you <u>think</u> of mashed sprouts?"* ✓

Instead of asking,

✗ *"Were you pleased when you won the Trans-Siberian Pogo Stick Marathon?"*

ask,

✓ *"What were your <u>feelings</u> when you won the Trans-Siberian Pogo Stick Marathon?"*

> Aaaargh!

Writing Good Interview Answers

The other thing about an interview is that it's got to be <u>realistic</u>. Take a good look at these <u>glorious tips</u> to see how it's all done...

Pretend to be the Person that you're Interviewing

When you write the answers, <u>pretend</u> to be the person you've chosen and think how <u>they</u> would answer the question. Think about what things are important to <u>them</u>.

The most important thing for me is that the fans like the record. I'm doing it for my fans because they're the people I care about.

Write in the way they Speak

Don't just write <u>what</u> they would talk about. You've got to make it <u>sound</u> like them as well. Always try to write in the way that they <u>speak</u>.

Yeah, I was over the moon when we won the double in '95.

Oh, would I like to dine? I thought you said di<u>ve</u>.

Are you going to ask yes/no questions? — No...

So the thing to do is this — write how you'd talk if you were that person. Be formal if you're a politician. But most people <u>don't</u> talk like that — they say what they think. It's tough to write like that, but it's definitely worth the effort — it's the only way you'll get those <u>top marks</u>...

QUESTION-READING SKILLS

Doing Reading Questions

Don't go crashing straight in — have a <u>think</u> about what you're doing first. The next few dazzling pages are positively <u>brimming</u> with handy hints on how to <u>prepare</u> yourself for any reading questions that might come your way. Read, absorb and smile in anticipation...

Make sure you Read the papers Carefully

You'll get <u>two</u> test papers — one with a <u>story</u> and maybe some other bits to read, the other paper will have the wicked <u>questions</u> in it.
Before you start, you must read through the paper with the story.
Don't leave a single <u>weeny</u> thing out.

> Always read carefully through
> the story paper before you start

Work out what the Question is Asking

All the questions will be about the stuff you've just read. You must read very <u>carefully</u> through each question before you even think about answering it. Always remember the magic question:

What is it asking me to do?

What happened to Ewan after he ran away?

This is asking you to <u>explain</u> a bit of the story.

Find four phrases that let us know we are about to read a strange and mysterious story.

It's asking you to find <u>four</u> phrases for 'strange and mysterious' in the story.

You absolutely must Answer the Question

Make sure your answer matches what you're asked to do. It's easy to slip up in this way.

> Write <u>clear</u> answers
> and <u>give reasons</u> to
> back them up.

Read both papers — I like the sports section...

Your step by step guide to tackling those reading questions... Step 1: <u>chill out</u>. Step 2: check out <u>both</u> papers and let it all sink in. Step 3: hmm OK now <u>answer</u> those blinking questions...

Working Out The Answers

Heh heh — this is where the <u>fun</u> starts...
You've worked out <u>what</u> it's on about — so time to go fishing for that slippery little <u>answer</u>...

Always try to Find the answer in the Passage

Sometimes the question will tell you exactly where to look for the answer.

The young girl decided to keep the pearl. What then happened to her because of this decision?

> This suggests that the answer comes near the bit where the girl decides to keep the pearl.

There'll always be information in the passage to help you answer the question.
You've just got to know where to look.

Sometimes you have to Work Out the answer

Watch out — this is the really tricky part. For some questions, the answer isn't obvious or clear. Instead <u>you</u> have to find the right bits to help you <u>work out</u> what the answer should be.

Lions and tigers are similar in many ways. Write down three ways they are similar.

① First read the bit in the passage about lions — think about what it says about lions.

② Then read the bit about tigers — think what it says about tigers.

③ Find three similarities from what you've read.

④ If you can't think of three, just read it again.

Now remember — don't make the answers up.
You've got to find things which really are from the passage.

Look out — there's an answer about...

<u>Don't</u> chuck in the towel after one half-baked <u>skim-read</u>... it's in there <u>somewhere</u> — even if it's not obvious. Go through with a fine-tooth comb for <u>anything</u> vaguely to do with the <u>question</u>... then put the bits <u>together</u>. It's a bit of work, but do it and the marks will come rolling in...

How to Give a Good Answer

It's another stonker of a page. <u>Everything</u> you ever wanted to know about writing <u>clear</u>
<u>answers</u>. This is the real <u>meaty</u> bit, so don't bale out yet...

Some questions are about Words and Phrases used

Some questions ask you to find particular words and phrases used in the passage — which is
pretty easy, really. Just remember:

> Copy out the phrase exactly
> and put it in speech marks.

The speech marks show it comes from the passage.

Other Questions need answers in Your Own Words

When you answer a question in your own words, it is also important to give the bit of the
passage that gave you the answer. This shows how you got your answer and that you haven't
just made it up.

> <u>Back up</u> your answer using
> bits from the passage.

> **Remember:**
> If you use any exact words
> or phrases from the story,
> put them in <u>speech marks</u>
> (see p.14).

What happened after John ate the mouldy food?

This bit is from the actual passage.

John started to feel ill. The passage says, "He felt like he was going to be sick."

This is the answer in your own words.

Don't forget the
speech marks.

Put it another way — use your own words...

There it is in a nutshell — how to tackle the <u>three different sorts</u> of questions. Good, eh.
<u>Copy out</u> bits, <u>answer</u> in your own words or <u>back up</u> your own ideas with bits from the story.

Questions that Ask What You Think

<u>Hang on</u> in there — nearly done. It's no picnic, but it's <u>not as bad</u> as it seems. They want to know what <u>you</u> think — so tell them. In graphic detail. And tell them <u>why</u>.

'How' and 'Why' Questions often ask what You Think

Some cunning questions ask you to write what you think about the passage, and to give reasons from the passage to back up what you've said.

How do you think Jean felt when she found out she couldn't go on the trip?

This is asking for your opinion, <u>but</u> the trick is to find bits in the passage which support your opinion.

Never ever put down the first thing that comes into your head. <u>Give proper reasons</u> for what you write, not just guesses.

Why were the children cheering and laughing when they reached the sea?

Here, you must <u>give reasons</u> for what the children were doing, based on what you've read.

Give your Opinion — and then Explain it

1) With some easy questions, you'll find clear bits in the passage that back up your opinion — and <u>please</u> don't forget the speech marks in your answer. Then you need to explain <u>how</u> these bits back up what you've written.

> *I think Jean felt sad because in the second paragraph it says that: "her eyes were red, as if she had been crying."*

2) Unfortunately, some really horrible questions <u>don't</u> give any clear reasons in the passage.

Did you enjoy this story? Give reasons for your opinion.

Just put what <u>you think</u> here — but once again, give reasons for your opinion. Make absolutely sure you <u>never</u> give reasons like, "it was boring." You've got to explain <u>why</u> it was boring.

I'll give you an onion — oh, you said opinion...

You <u>know</u> if you write anything like, "It was boring and I hated it," you're asking for trouble. You've read the page, you know what to do — say <u>why</u> it was naff, scary, exciting or whatever. <u>Pin down</u> those crafty little <u>marks</u> then sit and have a good old chuckle to yourself.

EXAMPLE TEST STORY

Reading Test — Story

Right — time to look at a practice <u>Reading paper</u>. You need to <u>read the whole thing</u> through first, with the questions as well — they're on p.56 & 57.

Robin Hood and the Archery Contest

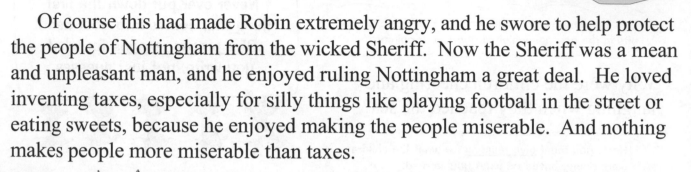

Long ago in Sherwood Forest, there lived a man you may have heard of, called Robin Hood. Years before, he had been driven into the Forest by the Sheriff of Nottingham, who had stolen his land and burnt his father's castle.

Of course this had made Robin extremely angry, and he swore to help protect the people of Nottingham from the wicked Sheriff. Now the Sheriff was a mean and unpleasant man, and he enjoyed ruling Nottingham a great deal. He loved inventing taxes, especially for silly things like playing football in the street or eating sweets, because he enjoyed making the people miserable. And nothing makes people more miserable than taxes.

Nobody agreed with the taxes, but everyone had to pay them. Once some brave people refused to pay, but the Sheriff sent his soldiers to arrest them and put them in prison. Then he took their money anyway.

When he had collected all the money from a new tax, the Sheriff would send some of it to London, to the Royal Treasury. Unfortunately for him, the only road to London passed through Sherwood Forest. Every time the Sheriff sent money, Robin Hood and his gang would ambush the soldiers carrying it and steal the whole lot. Then they would ride around the countryside, giving the money straight back to the same people it had been collected from!

The people loved Robin Hood; "He's the only person who ever helped us," they used to say. "He will keep us safe from the Sheriff. We hate the Sheriff and his taxes!"

When the Sheriff heard this, it made him turn red with anger. He would go away and think up more silly taxes. While he was inventing them, he would also be thinking about ways to capture Robin Hood.

One day though, the Sheriff had a brilliant idea.

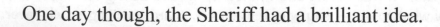

Reading Test — Story

He called for his advisors and explained the idea to them.

"The people think that Robin Hood is a hero. They say he is the best archer in the world. So why don't we challenge him to prove it? Let's have an archery contest. The winner will be presented with a golden arrow."

"But what good will that do?" asked one of the Sheriff's advisors.

"Fool!" muttered the Sheriff. "It'll be a challenge to Robin Hood. He won't be able to resist coming to the contest. All we have to do is make sure he wins. When I present him with the golden arrow, we'll have soldiers hidden all around, waiting to arrest him. He won't be able to escape!" The Sheriff laughed cruelly.

What are you lot looking at?

What the Sheriff didn't know was that someone else had heard the conversation. The King's cousin, Maid Marion, had been brought to Nottingham Castle when the King left on Crusade. She was a brave, clever woman, who had been friends with Robin Hood before he became an outlaw.

She had been listening at the door to the Sheriff's throne room. As soon as she heard what the Sheriff was planning, she ran back to her bedroom.

Shusssh!

"I must be quick!" she thought, and she rummaged through her wardrobe until she found a tatty old robe. Quickly she put this over her fine silk dress. The robe was prickly and made her skin itch, like a new jumper, but she didn't care. She knew what she had to do.

Picking up a bundle of dirty clothes, she bent over forwards so that she could walk like an old woman. Now she was ready to find Robin.

Her disguise worked perfectly. None of the guards suspected an old washerwoman, so they let her out of the Castle. Once she was out of sight she left her bundle in a hedge and ran as fast as she could to Sherwood Forest.

Inside the Forest it was dark and cold. Marion could hardly see a thing so she had to go slowly. All around her there were rustling noises, as if she was being followed by a pack of wild animals. She started to feel a bit scared.

Reading Test — Story

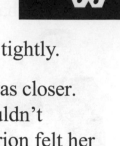

"Robin!" she called faintly, but there was no reply.

Suddenly she heard a blood-curdling howl from far off. A wolf! Marion shivered and looked around her. She still couldn't see anything. She stooped down and picked up a stick from the ground, ready to fight. Her hands shook with fear.

"I must go on," she told herself bravely, and gripped the stick tightly.

She heard another howl, but this time it was closer. Marion froze. She was so afraid that she couldn't move her legs. Another howl, and now Marion felt her spine tingle in horror. Faintly, from the other direction, she heard a new sound. It was an answering howl.

Then the air was filled with a great hooting sound. A hunting horn! The howls stopped. There was a sudden gust of air as a figure seemed to swoop down from the trees, swinging on a long rope.

"Marion!" cried Robin Hood, and smiled. "I didn't recognise you in that disguise. But what's wrong? What are you doing alone in Sherwood Forest?"

"I came to warn you!" said Marion. "The Sheriff is holding an archery contest tomorrow. He wants you to enter. It's a trap, Robin!"

Robin put his head on one side and thought for a moment. "A trap, is it?" Then he grinned. "We can't disappoint the Sheriff then!"

"But it's too dangerous!" said Marion.

"Don't worry," answered Robin. "I have a plan too!"

Marion returned to the Castle, but she didn't sleep a wink all night. She was worried about the Sheriff's trap, but she knew that Robin was as stubborn as she was. There was no way he would miss the contest for anything.

The day of the contest arrived, and a huge crowd gathered on the field outside the city where the archery range had been set up. There were people laughing and cheering, tradesmen selling hot pies and toffee apples, and even a group of travelling clowns.

Reading Test — Story

The Sheriff sat on a platform at one end of the field, with the golden arrow in front of him. Beside him sat Marion, who was worried sick about Robin but trying hard to hide it from the Sheriff.

The Sheriff looked anxiously over the archers. Where was that villain Robin Hood? He was so close to capturing his enemy.

Marion watched the crowd too. Her heart was pounding inside her. Where was Robin? She looked behind the platform. There were soldiers everywhere.

The contest began, and the crowd cheered as the archers fired. Still there was no sign of Robin. The crowd became restless, waiting for their hero. They grew angry. "Where's Robin Hood?" they shouted. "What a coward!"

There was a great shout of laughter. An old beggar was fitting an arrow to his bow. The crowd thought it was very funny that a ragged old beggar had entered the contest and they teased him. The Sheriff smiled at how ridiculous the beggar looked, but Marion felt sorry for him. "I hope he does well just to prove them wrong," she thought.

The beggar fired. There was silence. He had hit the bull's-eye cleanly. Marion leapt to her feet and clapped. Slowly the crowd joined in. The beggar had won the contest.

The Sheriff couldn't believe it, but he realised he had to present the golden arrow. He could always have his men steal it back from the beggar later.

The beggar came up to the platform. "Well done," said the Sheriff rudely, handing over the golden arrow. As he did so, the beggar threw off his ragged cloak and grabbed the Sheriff by the scruff of the neck. It was Robin Hood.

The Sheriff stared in terror. He was very afraid of Robin close up. Even the hidden soldiers were scared. They didn't dare move in case Robin killed the Sheriff. "Thank you for my prize," laughed Robin.

He let go of the Sheriff and winked at Marion. Then he ran back down into the crowd. The Sheriff's men followed, but they couldn't find him anywhere. He had vanished back into Sherwood Forest along with the golden arrow, ready to fight the Sheriff again some other day.

Adapted from an old Nottingham folk tale.

56

Questions on the Story

Now it's time to look at a few questions about the <u>story</u> you've just read. Go through them carefully and you'll be all set to answer any reading questions that might come your way...

These questions are about the story *Robin Hood and the Archery Contest*.

1. What does the first paragraph of the story tell us?

This is the <u>title</u> of the page — make dead certain that the title of the questions is the <u>same</u> as the title of the story.

This one's a <u>multiple choice</u> question. You're given <u>four</u> possible answers, but only one is correct.

| that Robin Hood liked the Sheriff of Nottingham | that Robin was a rich and very powerful man | that Robin had lost his lands and lived in the Forest | that Robin Hood lived in Wales |

Be careful — there may be more than one true statement, but there's only <u>one</u> in the first paragraph.

(1 mark)

2. Put these events from the story in the right order by giving them a number from 1 to 5.

Go through the story slowly and work out which event on the list happened first, then what happened second, until you get to the fifth one.

_____ Robin grabbed the Sheriff by the scruff of the neck.

____2____ Marion went to the forest.

____1____ The Sheriff had an idea about how to trap Robin Hood.

_____ Robin Hood disappeared back into the Forest.

_____ A beggar won the archery contest.

(1 mark)

3. Why did the Sheriff want to hold an archery contest?

A much tougher question this — you need to find the bit in the story where the Sheriff is <u>talking</u> about the archery contest. Don't forget to back up what you write.

The Sheriff wanted Robin to enter the contest and win so that his men could capture him.

The Sheriff said it was a "challenge" that Robin wouldn't "be able to resist."

(1 mark)

More Questions on the Story

This is a trickier question — it's about the <u>words</u> and <u>phrases</u> used in the story.

4. List **two** ways in which the writer adds suspense to the story before the archery contest.

> For answering this one, you'll need to look at the bit of the story before the archery contest happens. Look at the way everything is <u>described</u> — you must find <u>two</u> ways.

<u>The story keeps saying that there was no sign of Robin Hood — it keeps asking "Where was Robin?"</u>

<u>This adds suspense because it makes you wonder if Robin really will come to the contest or not.</u>

<u>It says Marion was "worried" about Robin, which makes us worried too.</u>

(2 marks)

> This is the sort of answer they want — <u>two</u> clear answers backed up with <u>phrases from the story</u> (in speech marks), and an <u>explanation</u> for each answer.

5. Were you surprised when Robin appeared at the end of the story? Give **two** reasons for your answer.

> Here's one of those nasty questions that ask you about what <u>you think</u>. You'll have to work out <u>your own reasons</u> why — think about what you expected to happen at the end and why.

<u>I wasn't surprised at the end. You knew Robin would turn up because the hero always</u>

<u>arrives just in time in this kind of story. He also said he wouldn't disappoint the Sheriff.</u>

(2 marks)

> Watch out — you must give <u>two</u> reasons if you want to get the <u>two</u> marks.

6. Did you enjoy reading this story? Explain your opinion.

Yes No

> More opinions now — just keep in mind you get the marks for <u>backing up</u> what you write.

<u>I enjoyed reading the story because the horrible Sheriff got what he deserved and Robin</u>

<u>won the contest. It was obvious what would happen at the end but it was still good fun.</u>

(2 marks)

58

Reading Test — Poem

Poems are cool — they're just short pieces of writing that use lots of great-sounding words which makes them fun to read. They also use lots of <u>images</u> — images are words and phrases that give you a <u>picture</u> of an action or a thing, bringing it to life. Some images can have double meanings. Answering questions on poems is a dead tricky business so you need plenty of practice.

Windy Nights

Whenever the moon and stars are set,
Whenever the wind is high,
All night long in the dark and wet,
A man goes riding by.
Late in the night when the fires are out,
Why does he gallop and gallop about?

Whenever the trees are crying aloud,
And ships are tossed at sea,
By, on the highway, low and loud,
By at the gallop goes he.
By at the gallop he goes, and then
By he comes back at the gallop again.

Robert Louis Stevenson

Questions on the Poem

Don't forget to check that the title with the questions is the same as the one with the poem.

These questions are about the poem *Windy Nights*.

1. This poem is about a man riding his horse on stormy nights. Find **two** different words or phrases in the poem that describe how bad the weather was.

You've got to find two different parts of the poem that describe the storm. That means you can only pick out bits about the weather — not about how dark the night was.

1. *The wind is making a noise in the trees — "the trees are crying aloud".*

2. *It says that the night is "wet" which shows it has been raining.*

(1 mark)

The big problem with poem questions is that they look a lot tougher than they really are. Don't think about the fancy words — just about what the question is asking.

2. Find **two** pairs of rhyming words in the poem.

Rhymes happen when two words have an ending that sounds the same.

The words "set" and "wet" rhyme in the first part of the poem.

The words "sea" and "he" rhyme in the second part of the poem.

(1 mark)

This is the sort of answer they want — but don't forget the speech marks.

3. The word "gallop" is an important word in the poem. What does it make you think of when you read it?

Watch out — this is a really hard question. You need to say what you imagine when you read the word "gallop" and explain <u>why</u> it makes you think that.

The word "gallop" shows that the horse is going fast so it makes me think that

the rider is in a hurry. It's repeated a lot so it seems as if the horse never stops.

(2 marks)

Reading Test — Descriptions

You might get questions on a group of <u>short descriptions</u>. This is pretty <u>hard</u> — so just keep your eyes peeled and your brain on the job. The <u>secret</u> of writing <u>good answers</u> on a group of passages is knowing how to <u>compare</u> different bits.

Don't Go Near the Water

Sharks are amazing creatures. They are known as the deadliest hunters in the sea, with their long, torpedo-shaped bodies. In fact, many sharks are harmless, like the Basking shark, one of the largest of the shark family, which lives near the surface of the ocean and feeds on tiny sea creatures called plankton.

Most people think that real sharks are like the monster sharks in films and on television. Fortunately most are not, but there are some kinds of shark that can be just as dangerous.

> Look at these short descriptions of **three** kinds of shark.

The Great White Shark

Great Whites are one of the most feared creatures in the sea. They live in tropical and subtropical waters, and they can grow up to 9 metres long. Most Great Whites are actually grey, blue or brown with a white belly, and their powerful teeth are triangles with edges like saws. They have a crescent-shaped tail.

The Whale Shark

Whale sharks are the largest kind of shark in the world — up to 11 metres in length. They live in tropical waters all around the world, but they are not dangerous. Whale sharks are brown or grey with white or yellow stripes. They often travel near the surface of the sea.

The Mako Shark

Mako sharks are fierce predators. They come from the same family of sharks as the great white and they are especially fast — they can swim at speeds of up to 65 kilometres per hour. They are large blueish sharks found in the Atlantic, Pacific and Indian oceans. Mako sharks can grow up to 3 metres long.

Questions on Short Descriptions

Now look at these sample questions about the descriptions on the last page — and remember, you seriously do need to learn how to answer these kinds of question, so make sure it's sorted.

These questions are about the *Don't Go Near the Water* section.

1. Look at the descriptions of the Great White shark, the Whale shark and the Mako shark on p.60.

   Draw lines to match each creature to the words or phrases that describe them.

   One line has been drawn for you. Draw six more lines to match each creature to the correct descriptions.

Well this one shouldn't be too tricky — just keep this big warning in mind:
Always check the original description even if you think you know the answer.

Shark

Mako shark

Whale shark

Great White shark

Description

just lives in tropical waters

lives in Indian, Atlantic and Pacific oceans

has a crescent-shaped tail

swims at speeds of up to 65 kilometres per hour

lives in tropical and subtropical waters

only grows up to 3 metres long

travels near the surface of the sea

(3 marks)

2. Think about the three kinds of shark described on p.60.
   Which is the only one that human beings have **no** reason to fear?

It's getting tougher now — you need to think about each of the three sharks and whether the description says they are dangerous or not. Find the one that isn't and you've got your answer.

(1 mark)

Tricky Questions

Some of the questions you'll come across will be really <u>hard</u> — but not impossible. You'll just have to spend time <u>thinking</u> about them before you give an answer. Look at the <u>sample questions</u> on this page and learn how you need to answer them — get it clear in your mind now, because that's the only way you'll get the marks.

> These questions are about the introduction and short pieces called *Don't Go Near the Water* on p.60.

1. The introduction says that sharks are known for...

    ...their long, torpedo-shaped bodies.

    What is the effect of these words?

    > OK — this is an real stinker of a question. You've got to say what these words <u>make you think</u> about sharks, so look really closely at them. The phrase that jumps out at you is "torpedo-shaped". You need to say what effect comes from calling a shark "torpedo-shaped".

    The phrase "torpedo-shaped" makes sharks sound dangerous and fast like torpedoes.

    (1 mark)

2. Fill in the table to show which statements about the *Don't Go Near the Water* section are fact and which are opinion.

    > Right — here you need to look at each statement in turn, and ask yourself if they can definitely be proved by something in the passage, or whether they are just possibilities. Look at the answers below and see if you can work out why each one is a fact or an opinion.

	Fact	Opinion
These descriptions are frightening.		✓
Mako sharks are predators.	✓	
Sharks are like the monster sharks in films.		✓
Some sharks can be very dangerous.	✓	
Most Great Whites are grey, blue or brown.	✓	

(1 mark)

More Tricky Questions

<u>Watch out</u> for some of these questions — remember you just need to do <u>exactly</u> what the question asks you. They aren't trying to trick you — the secret is knowing what they want you to do. That means putting the <u>hard work</u> and <u>practice</u> in now, so you won't get caught out.

3. The title of the series of descriptions on p.60 is ***Don't Go Near the Water***. Why did the author choose this title?

Another shocker of a question here — this isn't as easy as it looks. If you write, "it tells you what it's about," you won't get any marks at all. You have to mention that sharks live in the water and are dangerous, and the title's a warning about the water — that's the only way to get <u>both</u> of the marks for this question.

The title is a warning not to go near the water because the passage is about sharks

— sharks are dangerous creatures that live in the water. The title grabs your attention too.

(2 marks)

<u>BIG TIP</u>: When they ask about titles, watch out for double meanings.

4. Using the information about Basking sharks in the first paragraph of ***Don't Go Near the Water***, write a description of the Basking shark to go with the other short pieces.

This is a sneaky little question — it's worth three marks, so you need at least three things about Basking sharks from the first paragraph. Then make your description look and sound like the other three descriptions on the page — just copy their style.

The Basking shark

Basking sharks are one of the largest species of shark. They tend to live near the surface of the ocean, but they are not dangerous. Basking sharks feed on small sea creatures called plankton.

(3 marks)

Tricky questions — knock knock, who's there...

Look at each question really blummin' <u>carefully</u> to work out <u>exactly</u> what it means. Be <u>ready</u> for the different <u>kinds</u> of question you get for stories, poems and descriptive writing. You'll find them all <u>bags easier</u> once you've got to grips with <u>all</u> the little handy <u>hints</u> in this section.

PRACTICE/PRACTISE
& ADVICE/ADVISE
# Practice/Practise & Advice/Advise

Some words are just plain <u>nasty</u>. They <u>sound</u> the same, but they're not <u>spelt</u> the same — just to get you flummoxed. You don't want to lose <u>marks</u> for bad spelling, so learn <u>all</u> these sneaky words.

Practise is a verb but Practice is a noun

These two words are a real pain — just remember, when you want a doing word use <u>practise</u> with an 's'. When you talk about an <u>event</u> or an <u>exercise</u> use <u>practice</u> with a 'c'. Don't get them wrong.

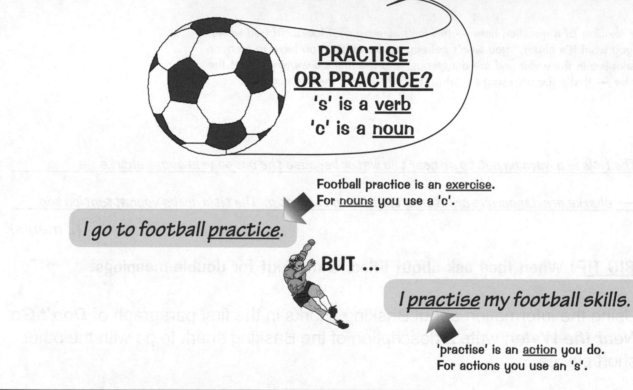

**PRACTISE
OR PRACTICE?**
's' is a <u>verb</u>
'c' is a <u>noun</u>

Football practice is an <u>exercise</u>.
For <u>nouns</u> you use a 'c'.

I go to football <u>practice</u>.

BUT ...

I <u>practise</u> my football skills.

'practise' is an <u>action</u> you do.
For actions you use an 's'.

It's the same as Advice and Advise

A good way of remembering whether to use an 's' or a 'c' is to think of <u>advise</u> and <u>advice</u>. Exactly the same rule applies to them. But they're easier to remember because they <u>sound different</u>.

Simon is <u>advising</u> Ricky.
It's an action he's doing — so it needs an 's'.

Perhaps you should see a doctor...

Simon <u>advised</u> Ricky to have the growth removed.
Ricky took Simon's <u>advice</u>.

Advice is <u>something</u> which Ricky gets from Simon.
It's a noun so you need a 'c'.

Take my advice — practice makes perfect...

I <u>still</u> have problems with these little tricksters. <u>Learn</u> the fiddly details of <u>when</u> to use which word, and always <u>check</u> through your writing for all these mistakes. It's the <u>only</u> way to make sure.

Affect/Effect & Passed/Past

When you <u>talk</u>, affect <u>sounds</u> just like effect. They're <u>different</u> words though, and they're very different when you <u>write</u> them down. Wrap your brain round these rules, and <u>save your marks</u>.

Affect is the Influencing Action, Effect is the Result

This one causes loads of mistakes, but it's really very simple once you know the rule.

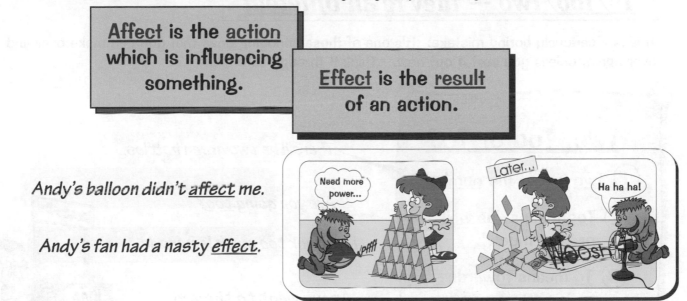

> **<u>Affect</u> is the <u>action</u> which is influencing something.**

> **<u>Effect</u> is the <u>result</u> of an action.**

Andy's balloon didn't <u>affect</u> me.

Andy's fan had a nasty <u>effect</u>.

Let it all sink in — affect is the influencing <u>action</u>, effect is the <u>result</u>. Oh and never confuse <u>infect</u> with affect or effect — infect is a totally different word to do with <u>illness</u>.

Don't confuse Passed with Past

Passed and past sound amazingly alike, but they're completely different words.

> **Passed with -ed is an <u>action</u>, but past with -t <u>is not</u>.**

I <u>passed</u> her on the way to school.
Mica <u>passed</u> the ball to Mel.

These are <u>actions</u>...

...but these <u>aren't</u>.

The garage is <u>past</u> the house.
They often played football in the <u>past</u>.

Remember — the secret is that passed with -ed is an action. So if it's <u>not an action word</u>, it must be <u>past</u>.

Special effects — when talking pigs fly past...

Keep a sharp look out for these ones. They're pretty tough to spot, because you <u>say</u> them just the <u>same</u>. Get these rules <u>firmly lodged</u> between your ears, or <u>bad spelling</u> = bye-bye <u>marks</u>.

To/Too/Two and Off/Of

Here are <u>two more</u> sets of cheeky little words to get your head round. You've just got to <u>learn</u> them.

More confusing words that Sound the Same

To/Too/Two — they're all Different

This is a seriously boring mistake. It's one of those annoying ones that you can make over and over again, unless you sort it out now. Think it through carefully:

Two, Too or To?

① <u>Two</u> is just the <u>number</u>.

② <u>Too</u> means "as well" or "<u>too</u> much".

③ <u>To</u> means <u>towards</u> or is <u>part of a verb</u>.

There'll be <u>two</u> green bottles.

Are you going <u>too</u>?

I've drunk <u>too</u> much lemonade.

Angus went <u>to</u> the zoo.

She decided <u>to</u> sing.

Off/Of — Two cunning Little Jokers

Another big-time mistake here — it's a bit of a teaser.
Get it into your head that 'off' is away <u>from</u> and 'of' is a linking word.

Time for take-off

This means flying <u>away from</u>.

Twenty percent off

This means <u>away from</u> the price.

You only need to learn that 'off' means away from. The rest of the time just use 'of'.

He's a friend <u>of</u> mine.

<u>Of</u> links the words together.

We were full <u>of</u> chocolate.

<u>Off</u> is like "away from".

<u>Of</u> is just a linking word.

Two more to learn — too important to forget...

These little jokers are definitely worth <u>learning</u>, so keep going over them till you could write them out in your <u>sleep</u>. Know them well enough to <u>spot</u> them a mile off when you <u>check</u> your writing.

Three Big Mistakes to Avoid

Pin back your lug-holes — these are some of the <u>trickiest</u> words around. Get them <u>all learned</u>.

Should have / Would have / Might have — NOT of

Whatever you do, you must drill this rule into your brain so it stays there forever.

<u>Never</u> use 'of' with <u>could</u>, <u>would</u>, <u>should</u> or <u>might</u>. Always use 'have' instead.
So you'd write "I could have", <u>never</u> "I could of"

> I <u>could have</u> been an astronaut.

> Sally <u>would have</u> made a good leader.

'might of' / 'could of'
'would of' / 'should of' ✗

'might have'
'could have'
'would have'
'should have' ✓

Where/Were/Wear — Wake up and Learn Them

① <u>Where</u> is used for places and positions.

> <u>Where</u> is the front door?

② <u>Were</u> is the past form of are.

> We <u>were</u> only borrowing the cat.

If it still makes sense when you use "<u>are</u>" instead, then it should be "<u>were</u>".

③ <u>Wear</u> is what you do with your clothes, hair and jewels — you <u>wear</u> them.

> My aunt likes to <u>wear</u> a helmet in the house.

All these words sound similar, but <u>where</u> goes with <u>places</u>, <u>were</u> is like <u>are</u>, and <u>wear</u> goes with <u>clothes</u>. Now make sure you learn them.

There/Their/They're — Three Awkward Words

Yep, here's three more classic problem words. They sound the same, but you don't write them the same. Get them sorted once and for all.

① <u>There</u> goes with <u>where</u> — it's about places.
② <u>Their</u> means <u>it belongs to them</u>.
③ <u>They're</u> is short for "<u>they are</u>".

You went <u>there</u>.

This is <u>their</u> house.

<u>They're</u> friendly people.

They're over there — in their pyjamas...

Time to get your brain in gear pal. This <u>really</u> needs to find a home between your ears. These are words you use <u>all</u> the time, so <u>learn</u> the <u>rules</u> or you'll make absolutely truckloads of <u>mistakes</u>.

Did or Done, Saw or Seen

Done and did, saw and seen — don't mix them up. If you use the wrong word in your writing then you'll be waving juicy marks goodbye. Don't get caught out — get learning.

Never write Done when you Really Mean Did

People are forever writing 'I done' in their stories and letters. The big problem is it's wrong. There are two ways of saying you did something in the past — I did or I have done.

> I did my homework. **OR** I have done my homework.

> We did what we were told.
> **OR** We have done what we were told.

> Shirley has done her best.
> Matt had done the crime.
> Jake did his shopping.

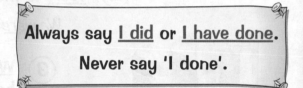

Done always goes
with has, have or had.
Did always goes
on its own.

Sometimes you can write has, have or had with an extra word before the done — but you still have to use both parts in the sentence.

> I have recently done something clever.
> He has always done his best.

Always say I did or I have done.
Never say 'I done'.

It's the same confusion with Saw and Seen

This is another dead common mistake. It's the same problem again — saw is a verb which makes sense on its own, but seen doesn't make sense without has, have or had.

> I saw that giant fly yesterday. **OR** I have seen the giant fly.

Never ever write 'I seen...' — you'll lose marks if you do.

Always say I saw or I have seen.
Never say 'I seen'.

Think about it — saw is a verb on its own, but seen always goes with has, have or had.

Done and dusted — now I've seen it all...

The stuff on this page might sound like a load of picky details, but you'll be doing yourself out of big family-sized portions of marks if you don't get it right. Don't say 'I done' or 'I seen'.

How to Use 'Who' and 'Which'

Getting these <u>two cheeky words</u> the wrong way round is an easy way to lose marks. It's <u>all</u> here on this page — so you've got <u>no</u> excuses... Get them <u>learned</u> and get more <u>marks</u>.

Use Who and Which to link two Actions

Who and which are two wonderful little words that you can use to <u>join</u> two actions. You need them when something has an action <u>done to it</u> in one part of a sentence, but also <u>does</u> an action in the other part.

'Who' is used with People

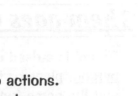

Leanne was a girl <u>who</u> knew what she wanted.

We use '<u>who</u>' here because we're talking about Leanne, who is a <u>person</u>.

'Which' is used with Everything Else

For anything which is not a person, like an <u>animal</u> or a <u>thing</u>, you use '<u>which</u>' instead of 'who'. You really must remember that, I'm afraid. Here's a couple of examples to get your brain in gear...

Bruno bought a kitten <u>which</u> ate everyone it saw.

'<u>Which</u>' is used here because we're talking about a <u>cat</u>, not a person.

My Dad only has two hairs <u>which</u> he combs over his head.

You sometimes have to be careful — '<u>which</u>' goes with '<u>hairs</u>' here, even though 'Dad' is doing both actions.

Using WHO to join actions — I'd use GLUE...

It's <u>so</u> easy to get these two mixed up — and it's another one of those dreaded <u>mark-drainers</u>. Best make sure <u>you don't</u> — cast your beady eye over this page till it's <u>firmly lodged</u> in your skull.

THEM AND THOSE	# When to Use 'Them' and 'Those'

Let's get this straight — if you get '<u>them</u>' and '<u>those</u>' muddled you will be losing <u>marks</u>. Lots of people use these words <u>differently</u>, but when you're being <u>marked</u>, this is the way to do it.

Them goes On Its Own

'Them' is a dead cool word — it's a <u>pronoun</u> (see p.2). 'Them' is used instead of a <u>plural name</u>, <u>person</u>, <u>place</u> or <u>thing</u> — it saves you having to repeat the name again. <u>Never</u> ever write 'them' and the name together. That's just <u>wrong</u> — get it hammered into your brain right away.

I went to school with the leopards.

OR   *I went to school with <u>them</u>.*

You and I can beat Greg and Tim.

         OR   *You and I can beat <u>them</u>.*

<u>Don't ever</u> write anything like "I went to school with them leopards", or "Pass me them books." It's just wrong. If you write something like "them books" you'll <u>lose</u> marks.

Don't use Them when you mean Those

When you write a sentence pointing something out, <u>don't</u> use 'them' — you've got to use 'those' instead. Just remember — if you're writing the <u>name</u> of the thing use '<u>those</u>' not 'them'.

Pass me one of <u>those</u> hooks.

<u>Those</u> worms look tasty.

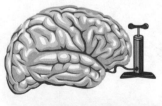

Once you get it pumped into your brain, you can't go wrong.

Pass me <u>those sausages</u>.   *Pass <u>them</u> to me.*

Those tricky words — I love them...

It's not about whether you "speak proper", it's just about making sure you don't <u>lose</u> precious <u>marks</u>. It boils down to this — <u>don't</u> write "<u>them books</u>" or "<u>them earwigs</u>" or whatever.

Make Your Handwriting Better

If your work looks like Egyptian hieroglyphics or like an inky spider's crawled about, <u>no-one</u> will be able to <u>read</u> it. It's really important that you keep your <u>handwriting tidy</u> so <u>take care</u> and <u>don't rush</u>.

Don't be Fancy, just be Neat

It's <u>not</u> a good plan to be really <u>fancy</u> with your writing. Curly bits get in the way and make your writing <u>hard</u> to read. Keep things nice and <u>simple</u> so you don't miss out on any <u>marks</u>.

Keep it neat.

Don't muck about with fancy <u>curly bits</u>.
Don't put <u>circles</u> above the letter i — just <u>dots</u>.

Keep it <u>simple</u> and keep it <u>neat</u>.

Get your Spacing Right

Make sure everything is in the <u>right place</u> when you write, as well as each word being <u>neat</u> on its own. There are two things to watch out for.

Make sure the <u>spaces</u> between your words are all the <u>same size</u>.

Keep your writing on the line. Don't let it float above or below.

If your writing does float off, it'll look <u>scruffy</u>, it'll be <u>harder</u> to <u>read</u>, and it might get <u>tangled up</u> in the line above or below. That's bad news. So don't let it happen.

Teacher, teacher, there's a spider in my ink...

You don't need to do anything <u>fancy</u> — just keep your writing <u>neat</u> and make sure you don't drift off the <u>line</u>. That way no-one will miss out on all that <u>fantastic</u> stuff you're writing...

WORD BUILDING	**Two Spelling Tips**

The right <u>letters</u> in the right <u>order</u> — that's what good spelling is all about. You'll <u>lose</u> a whole bundle of <u>marks</u> if you get this wrong. Start with these <u>two tips</u>.

Break Words Up into Chunks

You can break up <u>longer words</u> into <u>chunks</u> called <u>syllables</u>. This makes them bags <u>easier to spell</u>.

Look out for words that are made up of two words joined together, e.g.
newspaper   handwriting

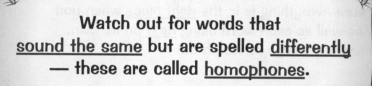

inside = in + side

careless = care + less

wondering = won + der + ing

Look Out for Words that Sound the Same

I'm still learning to spell

Watch out for words that <u>sound the same</u> but are spelled <u>differently</u> — these are called <u>homophones</u>.

 <u>Hair</u> sounds the same as <u>hare</u>

 <u>Deer</u> sounds the same as <u>dear</u>

<u>Knight</u> sounds the same as <u>night</u>

A syllable — not a stupid male cow...

You can't just throw a <u>jumble</u> of letters onto the page and expect people to read it. You don't want to miss out on any lovely marks, so make sure your spelling's up to scratch. Watch out for <u>tricky</u> words that are just <u>two little words</u> stuck together. Think in <u>chunks</u> when you <u>write</u> too.

Spelling Words With 'ie' or 'ei'

The i Before e Rule

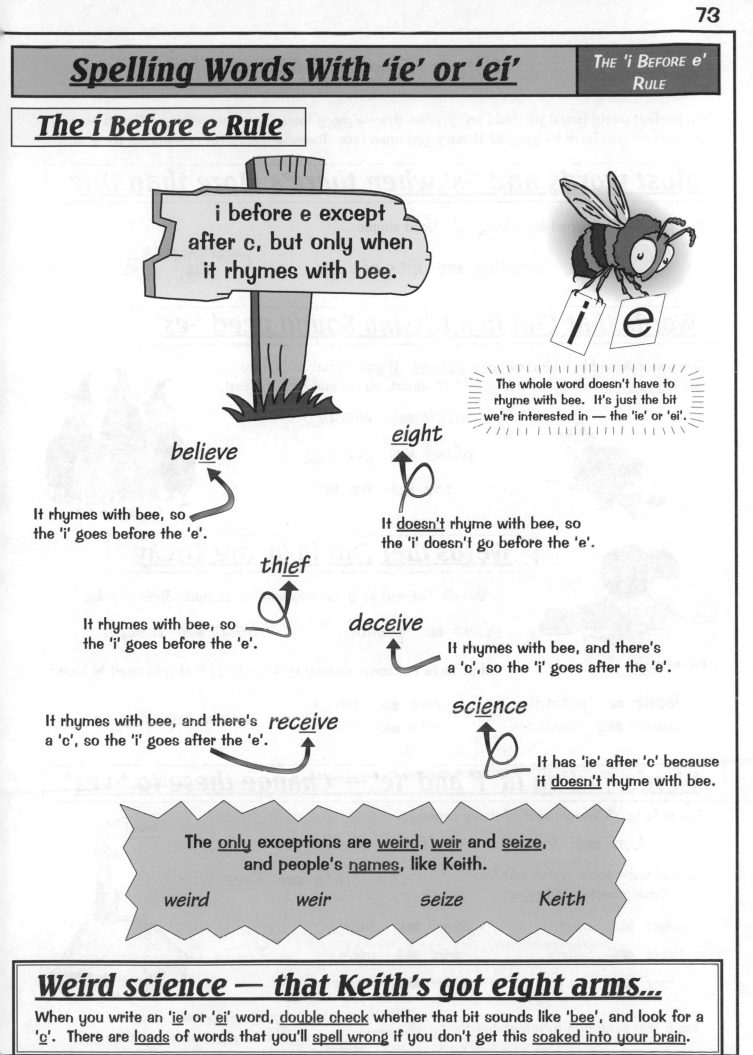

i before e except after c, but only when it rhymes with bee.

The whole word doesn't have to rhyme with bee. It's just the bit we're interested in — the 'ie' or 'ei'.

believe

It rhymes with bee, so the 'i' goes before the 'e'.

eight

It <u>doesn't</u> rhyme with bee, so the 'i' doesn't go before the 'e'.

thief

It rhymes with bee, so the 'i' goes before the 'e'.

deceive

It rhymes with bee, and there's a 'c', so the 'i' goes after the 'e'.

receive

It rhymes with bee, and there's a 'c', so the 'i' goes after the 'e'.

science

It has 'ie' after 'c' because it <u>doesn't</u> rhyme with bee.

The <u>only</u> exceptions are <u>weird</u>, <u>weir</u> and <u>seize</u>, and people's <u>names</u>, like Keith.

weird   weir   seize   Keith

Weird science — that Keith's got eight arms...

When you write an '<u>ie</u>' or '<u>ei</u>' word, <u>double check</u> whether that bit sounds like '<u>bee</u>', and look for a '<u>c</u>'. There are <u>loads</u> of words that you'll <u>spell wrong</u> if you don't get this <u>soaked into your brain</u>.

| PLURAL SPELLINGS | # When There's More Than One |

In a perfect world you'd just add an '<u>s</u>' when there's <u>more</u> than <u>one</u> of something. That'd be way <u>too easy</u> — you have to <u>learn</u> all these <u>weird</u> ones too. There're <u>marks</u> for <u>spelling</u> up for grabs.

Most words add '-s' when there's More than One

<u>Most</u> plurals are formed by adding '<u>-s</u>'. Dead simple...

one <u>bug</u> ➡ lots of <u>bugs</u>

Words that End in a Hissing Sound need '-es'

Some words end in a kind of <u>hissing sound</u>. If you added an '<u>s</u>' you <u>wouldn't hear it</u> on top of the '<u>s</u>' or '<u>sh</u>' sound, so we add '<u>-es</u>' instead.

witch ➡ witch<u>es</u>

glass ➡ glass<u>es</u>

fox ➡ fox<u>es</u>

Words that End in 'o' are Tricky

Words that end in '<u>o</u>' usually add '<u>-s</u>' to make their plural...

piano ➡ piano<u>s</u>   disco ➡ disco<u>s</u>

He had tomatoes for eyes

...but there are some sneaky <u>odd ones out</u> that you need to learn:

potato ➡ potato<u>es</u>   hero ➡ hero<u>es</u>

tomato ➡ tomato<u>es</u>   echo ➡ echo<u>es</u>   domino ➡ domino<u>es</u>

Words Ending in 'f' and 'fe' — Change these to '-ves'

I'm sure you'll know most of these already...

loaf ➡ loa<u>ves</u>   shelf ➡ shel<u>ves</u>

...but once again watch out for those cheeky <u>odd ones</u>:

life ➡ li<u>ves</u>

chief ➡ chief<u>s</u>   dwarf ➡ dwarf<u>s</u>

belief ➡ belief<u>s</u>   grief ➡ grief<u>s</u>

roof ➡ roof<u>s</u>   proof ➡ proof<u>s</u>

Darn!

Try a silly sentence to remember them.   It gave the <u>chief grief</u> that there was no <u>proof</u> that the <u>dwarf</u> had been on the <u>roof</u>.

When There's More Than One

Words that End in 'y'

This needs a bit of thought. Some of these words take '-s' to make the plural.
Others change the 'y' to 'ies'. You just have to look at the letter before the 'y':

> If the letter before the 'y' is a vowel, then just add 's' for the plural. If the letter before the 'y' is a consonant, the 'y' becomes 'ies' for the plural.

A vowel is one of these: a e i o u. Anything else is a consonant.

Confused? Check out these examples:

this letter is a vowel

t**o**y ➡ toy**s**   just add 's'

I hate daisies

this letter is a consonant

dai**s**y ➡ dais**ies**   change 'y' to 'ies'

Watch out, though — names that end in 'y' just take 's' for the plural.

We went on holiday with the Kennedy family.
*We went on holiday with the Kennedy**s**.*

Please pass the sun lotion, Mrs Kennedy.

Words with Completely Different Plurals

Piranhas have very sharp teeth

These all change the vowel sound at the end.
You'll have to remember them, I'm afraid.

m**a**n ➡ m**e**n   wom**a**n ➡ wom**e**n

t**oo**th ➡ t**ee**th   g**oo**se ➡ g**ee**se

m**ou**se ➡ m**i**ce   oas**i**s ➡ oas**e**s

There's more than one 'more than one' rule...

A fair bit of stuff on these two pages then. The only way to learn it all is to take those lovely rules one at a time. The exceptions are just as important — make up some more silly sentences to get them all firmly lodged in your skull. Don't lose marks for bad spelling — get them learned.

Prefixes and Suffixes

The <u>meaning</u> of some words can be <u>changed</u> by <u>adding letters</u> to the <u>beginning</u> or <u>end</u> of the word. <u>Learn how this works</u> and it'll help your spelling...

Prefixes are Added to the Beginning of a Word

A <u>prefix</u> is a <u>group of letters</u> that is added to the <u>beginning of a word</u>.
Adding a <u>prefix changes</u> the <u>meaning</u> of the <u>original word</u>. Here are some examples...

This is the <u>prefix</u> → (un)tidy

Adding the 'un-' to 'tidy' <u>changes</u> the meaning to '<u>not tidy</u>'.

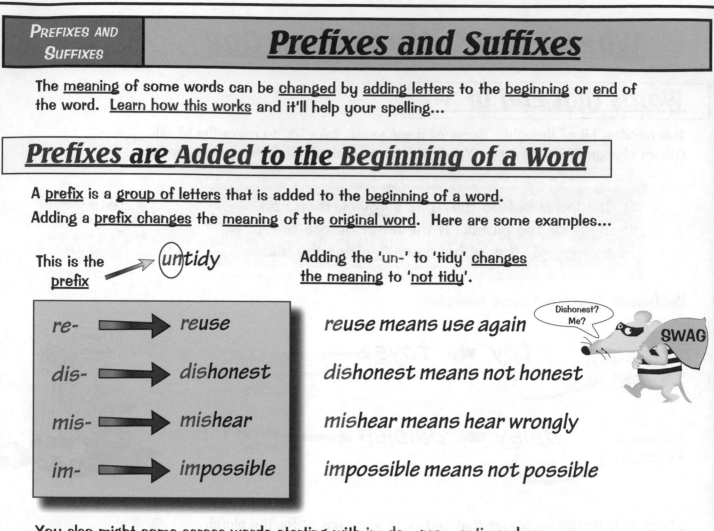

re- ⟶ reuse   reuse means use again

dis- ⟶ dishonest   dishonest means not honest

mis- ⟶ mishear   mishear means hear wrongly

im- ⟶ impossible   impossible means not possible

You also might come across words starting with <u>in</u>, <u>de-</u>, <u>pro-</u>, <u>anti-</u> and <u>ex-</u>.

Suffixes are Added to the End of a Word

A <u>suffix</u> is a <u>group of letters</u> that is added to the <u>end of a word</u>.
Adding a <u>suffix</u> also <u>changes</u> the <u>meaning</u> of the <u>original word</u>. Here are some examples...

tight(en) ← This is the <u>suffix</u>

Adding the '-en' to 'tight' <u>changes</u> the meaning to '<u>make more tight</u>'.

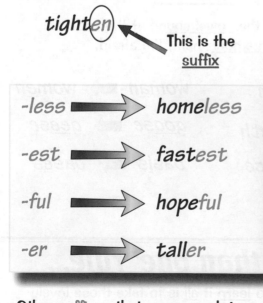

-less ⟶ homeless   homeless means without a home

-est ⟶ fastest   fastest means most fast

-ful ⟶ hopeful   hopeful means full of hope

-er ⟶ taller   taller means more tall

Other <u>suffixes</u> that crop up a lot are <u>-ive</u>, <u>-ible</u>, <u>-ness</u>, <u>-ing</u>, and <u>-al</u>.

Root Words

If you get good at spotting <u>prefixes</u> and <u>suffixes</u> you'll find it <u>dead helpful</u> when it comes to <u>spelling tricky words</u>. Here's how...

A Root Word is what a Prefix or Suffix is added to

The <u>root word</u> is the <u>basic word</u> that the <u>prefix</u> or <u>suffix</u> is added to.

If you can <u>break up a word</u> into a <u>root</u> word and a <u>prefix</u> or <u>suffix</u> you'll find it <u>loads easier to spell</u>.

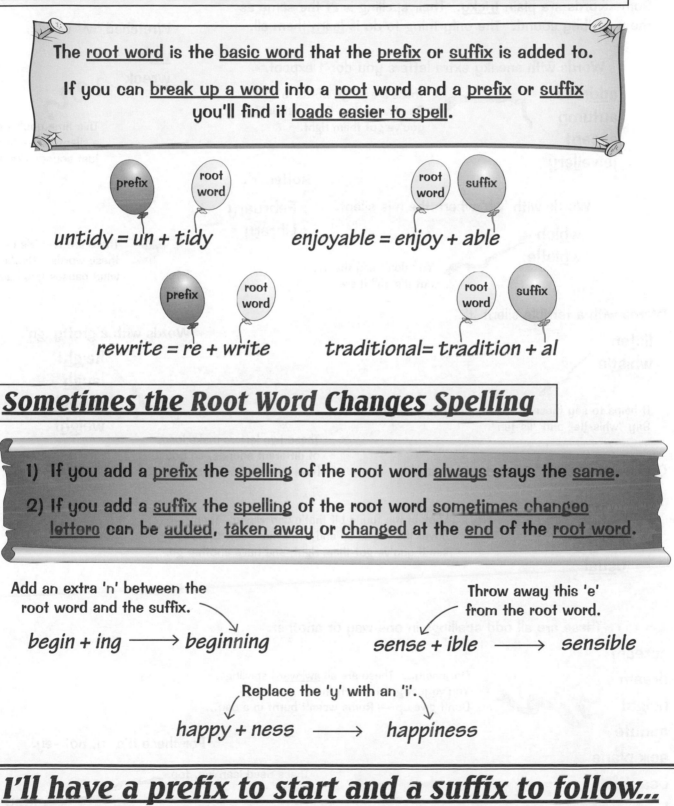

untidy = un + tidy

enjoyable = enjoy + able

rewrite = re + write

traditional = tradition + al

Sometimes the Root Word Changes Spelling

1) If you add a <u>prefix</u> the <u>spelling</u> of the root word <u>always</u> stays the <u>same</u>.

2) If you add a <u>suffix</u> the <u>spelling</u> of the root word <u>sometimes changes</u> — <u>letters</u> can be <u>added</u>, <u>taken away</u> or <u>changed</u> at the <u>end</u> of the <u>root word</u>.

Add an extra 'n' between the root word and the suffix.

begin + ing ⟶ beginning

Throw away this 'e' from the root word.

sense + ible ⟶ sensible

Replace the 'y' with an 'i'.

happy + ness ⟶ happiness

I'll have a prefix to start and a suffix to follow...

Prefixes and suffixes can be tricky. Watch out for those sneaky little <u>changes</u> to the <u>root word</u>. <u>Keep an eye out</u> for these words when you're <u>reading</u> and you'll soon get a feel for how things work.

AWKWARD VOWELS AND CONSONANTS

Difficult and Tricky Words

These little so-and-sos will trip you up big time if you don't learn 'em. <u>Look</u> at the word, <u>cover</u> it up, <u>write</u> it down and <u>check</u> the spelling. Get them right, and hold on to those <u>spelling marks</u>.

You Have to Learn these words

Some words are plain <u>tricky</u>. Their spelling isn't the same as the way they sound. The only thing to do is <u>learn</u> them all.

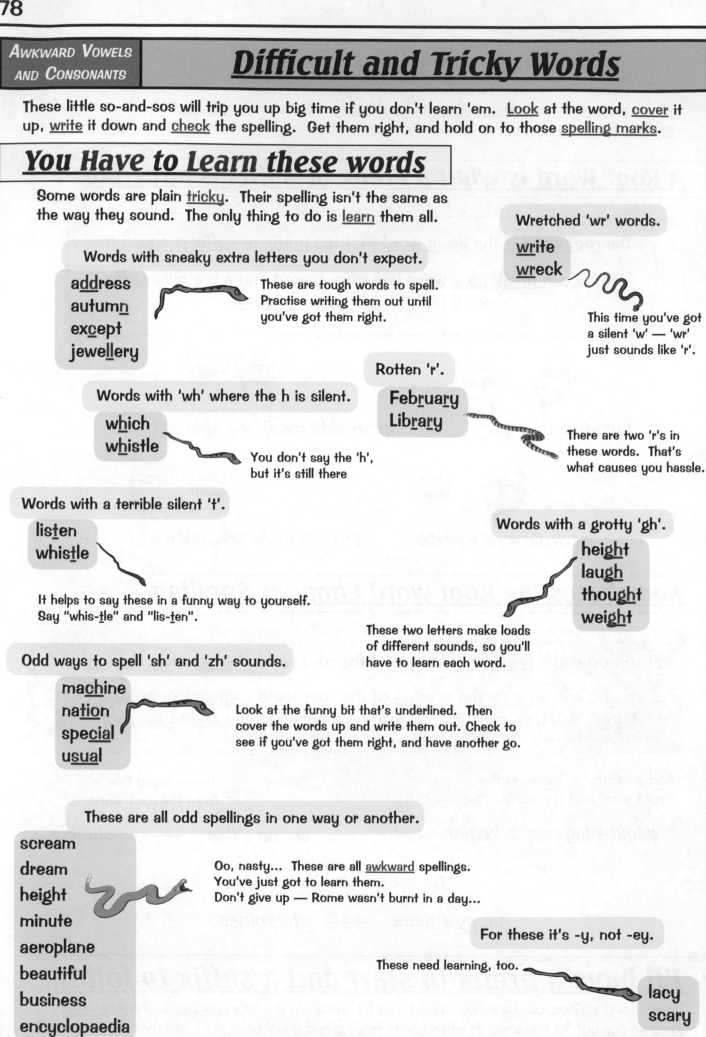

Words with sneaky extra letters you don't expect.

a<u>dd</u>ress
autum<u>n</u>
ex<u>c</u>ept
jewe<u>ll</u>ery

These are tough words to spell. Practise writing them out until you've got them right.

Wretched 'wr' words.

<u>wr</u>ite
<u>wr</u>eck

This time you've got a silent 'w' — 'wr' just sounds like 'r'.

Words with 'wh' where the h is silent.

w<u>h</u>ich
w<u>h</u>istle

You don't say the 'h', but it's still there

Rotten 'r'.

Feb<u>r</u>uary
Lib<u>r</u>ary

There are two 'r's in these words. That's what causes you hassle.

Words with a terrible silent 't'.

lis<u>t</u>en
whis<u>t</u>le

It helps to say these in a funny way to yourself. Say "whis-<u>t</u>le" and "lis-<u>t</u>en".

Words with a grotty 'gh'.

hei<u>gh</u>t
lau<u>gh</u>
thou<u>gh</u>t
wei<u>gh</u>t

These two letters make loads of different sounds, so you'll have to learn each word.

Odd ways to spell 'sh' and 'zh' sounds.

ma<u>ch</u>ine
na<u>ti</u>on
spe<u>ci</u>al
u<u>s</u>ual

Look at the funny bit that's underlined. Then cover the words up and write them out. Check to see if you've got them right, and have another go.

These are all odd spellings in one way or another.

scream
dream
height
minute
aeroplane
beautiful
business
encyclopaedia

Oo, nasty... These are all <u>awkward</u> spellings. You've just got to learn them. Don't give up — Rome wasn't burnt in a day...

For these it's -y, not -ey.

These need learning, too.

lacy
scary

Index